The 3 Obstacles

How to identify, overcome, and exploit them

James Ignizio, Ph.D.

The 3 Obstacles

Copyright © 2018, James Ignizio

All Rights Reserved.

CreateSpace Edition
In association with Bent Spur Press

Except as permitted under the United States Copyright Act of 1976, no part of this publication may be reproduced or distributed in any form by any means, or stored in a database or retrieval system, without prior written permission by the author. All trademarks are the property of their respective owners.

N022718/1013R

ISBN-13: 978-1986070256
ISBN-10: 1986070255

Table of Contents

TABLE OF CONTENTS III

PREFACE VII

1. INTRODUCTION 1

    Decisions, Decisions 3
    Science Trumps Fads 5
    Decision Types 10
    A Brief Introduction To The Three Obstacles 12

2. INDECISION, DECISIONS, AND ANALOGIES 15

    Success Achieved, Success Denied 20
    Analogies 26
    The Three Obstacles And Their Analogies 27
    Chapter Summary 31

3. UNNECESSARY COMPLEXITY 33

    The Yo-Yo Effect 37
    Up, Up And Away 40
    Unnecessary Complexity: A Definition 41
    Shopping In The Soviet Union 44
    Unnecessary Complexity And The IRS 45
    Unnecessary Complexity And National Defense 48
    Unnecessary Complexity And Tradition 50
    Walter Havisham Has His Problems 52
    The Crucial Importance Of Observation 56
    Chapter Summary 59

4. EXCESSIVE VARIABILITY 61

    Complexity's Impact On Variability 63
    Computation Of The Coefficient Of Variability 65
    Causes Of *Excessive* Variability 68
    Chapter Summary 77

5. INTELLECTUAL MYOPIA 79

- Attributes Of Decision-Makers ... 81
- Imagine That! ... 84
- Digitize This! ... 86
- I'll Think About That Tomorrow ... 87
- I Don't Care Syndrome ... 89
- One Plus One Is Not Necessarily Two ... 90
- Doubling Down ... 91

6. WEAPONIZATION OF THE THREE OBSTACLES ... 97

- The Fumblerooski ... 98
- WW2: North Africa Campaign ... 100
- The Business World ... 101
- Weaponization Of Revenue Generation ... 102
- Legal Documents ... 103
- Scientific Papers ... 104
- Politics ... 105
- Chapter Summary ... 107

7. FACTS ARE STUBBORN THINGS 109

- Miles Per Gallon? ... 113
- Fred Smith's Simple Little Problem ... 114
- Cycle Time Determination ... 116
- Increase Capacity (i.e., Throughput Flow) Or Reduce Variability? ... 119
- Wrong Assumptions In; Rubbish Out ... 121
- Don't Waste Your Time On Non-Constraints? ... 124
- Another Example Of *One Plus One Is Not Necessarily Two* ... 127
- Like Ripples On Water ... 130
- Difficult Decisions ... 131
- Chapter Summary ... 135

8. BAD NEWS ... 139

- Holistic *Versus* Atomistic ... 141
- An Offer You Can't Refuse? ... 145
- Black Teeth? ... 147

9. SUMMARY AND CONCLUSIONS ... 149

    Guidelines And Recommendations 150
    Too Much Of A "Good" Thing 151
    A Final Visit To The World Columbian Fair 153
    Conclusion 155

REFERENCES 157

ACKNOWLEDGEMENTS 163

ABOUT THE AUTHOR 165

Preface

*Nothing can be said to be certain
except death and taxes ... and bad decisions.*
— C. A. James

The achievement of any nontrivial goal (e.g., realization of a career choice, successful introduction of a product, selection of a weapon system, reduction of factory cycle time, enhancement of a supply chain's performance, change of a firm's mission statement, improvement of an organization's business processes, the hire of a key employee, adoption and implementation of a new policy, law, or regulation, etc.) requires the making of decisions. Every important decision, in turn, faces three major hurdles – *The Three Obstacles*. These are: *Unnecessary* Complexity, *Excessive* Variability, and *Intellectual Myopia*.

To successfully accomplish a given goal it is necessary to either eliminate or, at the very least, mitigate these obstacles. This elimination, or mitigation, can – as we shall learn – be most effectively addressed by means of a combination of *observation* and *science* coupled with a *holistic perspective*.

Observation, science, and a holistic perspective make it possible to enhance our decision-making skills

– and significantly improve their results – without having to resort to the adoption of fads and fashions, slogans, bumper stickers, motivational speakers, or – in particular – management gurus. And, while science provides the foundation for overcoming *The Three Obstacles*, the presentation that follows avoids the use of mathematics, scientific jargon, or stodgy case studies.

Ever wonder why such concepts as Lean, Six Sigma, Theory of Constraints, Business Process Reengineering, Total Quality Control, Just-in-Time, Management by Objectives, Balanced Scorecard, One Minute Management, etc., so often fail to provide satisfactory results or only achieve transient results – and just why their acknowledged failure and abandonment rate is so high (estimates range from 50 to 90 percent)? You'll discover the reason for these disappointing results in this book.

If you want to know how to avoid or overcome the limitations of the most popular and widely promoted management/self-help fads and fashions, you must learn how to either replace or, at the very least, augment those approaches with a firm knowledge and appreciation of *The Three Obstacles*. If you have a serious interest in obtaining a better understanding of how to significantly improve your probability of success in the decisions you make, and to recognize the hurdles you will face, read on.

1. Introduction

*It is dangerous to be right in matters on
which the established authorities are wrong.*
— Voltaire

The World Columbian Exposition, named in honor of Christopher Columbus, was set to take place in the city of Chicago in 1893. Also known as the Chicago's World Fair, the exposition was intended to introduce America – and the world – to the wonders of that age: including electricity and its applications. Two of America's most prominent firms, and fierce rivals, wanted to secure the contract to light that fair, a nighttime illumination effort that was to consist of nearly one hundred thousand lights – powered by the victor's generators.

Edison-General Electric proposed a direct current (DC) system while their competitor, Westinghouse, based theirs on the employment of alternating current (AC). The winner of the competition would not only receive enormous publicity, they would influence the all-important decision as to whether it would be Edison's DC or Westinghouse's AC electrical current system that would form the basis of the electrical grid necessary for the transmission of electricity throughout the nation.

Westinghouse's bid of $399,000 severely undercut that of Edison-General Electric and, to the dismay of Thomas Edison, Westinghouse won the contract. Westinghouse's plan was to use its AC system's generators to power the bulbs – all 100,000 of them – that were to be employed for the fair's nighttime illumination. The bulbs Westinghouse had planned to use were, however, *Edison bulbs*. Still seething at the loss of the contract to Westinghouse, Edison-General Electric banned their use by Westinghouse.

Westinghouse was, at that time, actually working on the design of its own light bulb ... but it had two significant drawbacks. First, it was neither as efficient nor long lasting as the Edison bulb. Second, and far more serious, it was constructed of one piece – *as was the Edison bulb* – and thus that one-piece design could be (and was) considered a patent infringement.

To avoid the matter of patent infringement, Westinghouse engineers designed a *two-piece* lamp. Instead of the *one-piece* Edison fused-glass seal, the new bulb used a ground glass "stopper" that was glued to the bulb's envelope. Voilà, *two* pieces!

While the new bulb solved the problem of patent infringement, it still had a much shorter expected lifetime (partially due to its two pieces) than an Edison bulb. That drawback was solved by manufacturing 250,000 of the bulbs – enough to fill the exposition's 100,000 sockets and replace any burnt-out bulbs over the six-month duration of the fair.

<<<<>>>>

The series of decisions made by George Westinghouse, his engineers, and patent lawyers served to overcome the enormous obstacles that had been placed between them and their goal of the accomplishment of the decision to pursue the contract to illuminate the World Columbian Exposition. While their story is unique, the obstacles that were faced were not. In every nontrivial decision, the same obstacles (i.e., *The Three Obstacles*) must be overcome, or at the very least mitigated, if a successful conclusion is to be reached.

Despite the omnipresent nature of *The Three Obstacles,* and the magnitude and extent of their impact, their existence is seldom noted, considered, or even explored – certainly not to the extent it should be. That, I believe, is the primary reason so many bad decisions are made, resulting in so many unfortunate endings. Once you have completed your reading of this book I'm confident you'll understand why.

I'll return to and elaborate on the Westinghouse-World Columbian Exposition story in Chapter 9. For now, however, let's consider the notion of *decisions* in more detail.

Decisions, Decisions

Whatever our station in life, we must make decisions. These range from the mundane:

- What should I have for breakfast?
- Should I take Interstate 35 into Austin this morning or the longer, but slightly less congested Route 183?

to vastly more complex and far-reaching matters such as:

- Should we adopt?

- What can be done to improve the performance of my business processes (or organization, military readiness, factory, production line, supply chain, competitive posture, product sales, etc.) and do so with minimal impact on morale (or cost, or time, etc.)?

- Should our next generation military jet fighter be designed to support as broad as possible a variety of roles (e.g., dog fighting, close air support, stealth and surveillance, electronic countermeasures, as well as support of *both* land-based and carrier-based takeoffs and landings) or should it be dedicated to a single purpose (e.g., for employment in close air support by a single branch of the military)?

Most of us wouldn't (I certainly hope) need to hire an expert for assistance in answering the first two questions. They require little thought and are amenable to "off-the-cuff" decisions (e.g., "I'll have what I've had for the last fifty years for breakfast: bacon, scrambled eggs over hard, and black coffee – and then I'll take Route 183 into Austin 'cause I'm sick and tired of being stuck in traffic on I-35.").

The consequences as a result of any decisions made in the last three instances are, on the other hand, vastly more important and far-reaching. In all five decisions, however, realize that our purpose (whether explicitly stated or not) is that of attaining some measure, or measures of "success" pertaining to the achievement of a specific goal.

Before proceeding further, it is vital to realize that "success" is not necessarily measured in terms of dollars and cents. Success, in this book, refers to the achievement of your goal, or goals – and these may be measured in terms of such notions as "satisfaction," e.g., the successful completion of a project, the accomplishment of a task, or the ability to avoid an adverse outcome.

Our focus will be on the decision-making involved in complex, far-reaching, and costly problems such as those encountered in seeking solutions to such matters as enhanced business processes, improved force readiness, more efficient production lines, weapons systems selection, introduction of new laws, policies, or regulations, more efficient hospital protocols, or superior financial planning. Our focus will not, however, be extended to the type of decision required in such very personal and highly emotional matters as "whether to adopt or not."

While one can predict the *expected* cost – in dollars and cents – of the adoption of a child (or, for that matter, a pet), there is simply no way to account for the emotions involved. The benefit, for example, of having your excited, tail-wagging, always delighted to see you dog meet you at the door each evening simply cannot be quantified.

As Clint Eastwood, in his role as *Dirty Harry*, said: "A man's got to know his limitations." I only wish that those who propose one after another "quick-and-easy, sure-fire scheme for decision-making" knew theirs.

Science Trumps Fads

The approach presented herein, unlike those proposed in most other books on managerial decision-making, or achieving success, is founded on observation and science, coupled with a holistic perspective. Rather than proposing a scheme in which to, for example, enhance business processes by means of such elusive if not abstract concepts as: reduce waste, enhance morale, reengineer the organization, manage by consensus, manage by walking around, benchmark, search for excellence, unleash your hidden strengths, or emulate Attila the Hun, I argue that the decision made should rely, in large part, on science.

The primary problem with the vast number of proposals for enhanced decision-making, or ways in which to achieve some measure of "success," is that they rely far too much on emotion – and, in particular, *promotion* – and far too little on science. Their claims of success are based on small sample sizes, a narrow perspective, emotional appeal, inherent biases, a limited observation period, and a fear of embarrassment (e.g., a majority of managers are, not surprisingly, reluctant to admit that the costly decision they made in the implementation of the "very latest" management fad did not really work out that well).

It should go without saying that it is important to be cautious before implementing any scheme that could result in a *negative* impact on you or your organization. Unfortunately, the adoption of a scheme based on glowing reports in the mass media (or even articles in highly regarded professional or trade journals) must be viewed with a degree of skepticism. Despite this, I've personally witnessed instances in which the CEO of a firm, a senior military officer, and a university president each devoted far more time on deciding the matter of the refurbishment of their offices than on the decision as to whether or not to adopt a current management fad for the solution of a major problem facing them in the performance of their firm, organization, or university.

Far too often, decisions as to the adoption of a given scheme are made solely on the basis of laudatory articles in the mass media or the salesmanship of a management guru. Just because the media or a consultant claims that some (supposedly) new scheme has resulted in a dramatic improvement, doesn't mean that the improvement isn't transient – or that the results claimed have not been exaggerated (or, as we'll see, that the scheme only tangentially focuses on but one of *The Three Obstacles*, while ignoring or even increasing the negative impact of the other two).

Consider, for example, the April 8, 2017 edition of the *Wall Street Journal* wherein Richard Harris reported the following [Harris, R. (2017)]:

- John Ioannidis (an epidemiologist and health-policy researcher at Stanford) concluded, after thoroughly investigating published results in his field, that *most published research findings are false.* [Allow me to reiterate: *most published research findings are false.* That conclusion definitely extends to the majority of claims made for management fads and fashions.]

- In 2011, scientists at Bayer published a paper in the journal *Nature Reviews Drug Discovery* showing that they could replicate only 25 percent of the findings of various discoveries. [The fundamental basis of the Scientific Method is that findings *must be able to be replicated.*]

- C. Glenn Begley, head of cancer research at Amgen, reported in the journal *Nature* that he and his colleagues could reproduce only six of 53 (i.e., just 11 percent) supposedly promising studies – even after enlisting help from some of the original scientists.

The claims of the vast and growing number of decision-making or decision support schemes proposed by a voracious horde of management gurus and self-help virtuosos are on far less solid ground than those of scientists involved in studies on the efficiencies (and side effects) of medicines and medical treatment. In many cases, however, alleged schemes for improvement in decision-making, organizational effectiveness, and the like are promoted by unsubstantiated claims, transient results, and dubious, non-replicable outcomes.

As just one example, consider my investigation of the performance improvement allegedly achieved by one of the seemingly never-ending "latest and greatest schemes for production line performance enhancement." I was invited to visit a firm's factory – one in which it was claimed that product cycle time (average time between the introduction of an unfinished part into the factory and its completion ... i.e., transformation into a finished product) had allegedly been reduced more than 40 percent by means of the introduction of a highly publicized, highly touted, and (at least for a few years) widely accepted scheme. The purported results had even appeared in the firm's press releases.

It took less than three hours to determine, conclusively, that the sole reason for the factory's reduction in cycle time was simply due to the fact that the facility had reduced its input (rate of the flow of raw materials into the factory) by approximately 60 percent. In other words, the load on the factory – *a primary determinant of cycle time* – had been substantially reduced. Simulations of the facility later showed that, *had the factory maintained its previous loading, its cycle time would not have improved ... at all*. My conclusion was reached based on science, not hype nor hope.

By the way, if anyone ever claims to have reduced cycle time (in a factory, supply chain, or business process), make sure that the results have been *load-adjusted*. Otherwise, the claim is absolutely and totally meaningless [Ignizio, J. P. (2009), pp.183-189].

Approximately six months after the above consultation, the same firm asked me to evaluate the results of their brand-new, state-of-the-art, latest and greatest predictive maintenance system. The system was designed to predict when and where the next *unscheduled* maintenance event would occur. It was actually quite good at that.

Unfortunately, the firm's maintenance specifications were poorly written (they were – like all too many maintenance specifications – *not* C4U-compliant, i.e., *not* **C**lear, **C**oncise, **C**omplete, **C**orrect, and **U**nambiguous). Consequently, while the predictive system itself was working quite well, the *improperly* written maintenance events (even though performed on the right components, at the right time) only served to *degrade* factory performance.

So, where do you think the firm placed the blame for their performance problems? You're right if you answered that it was erroneously and unfairly placed on the new predictive maintenance system. Such a *misassignment* of blame is, by the way, all too common. Rather than conducting a thorough investigation into the *actual* cause of the problem, the firm immediately jumped to the conclusion that the most recent change in their operating protocols (i.e., the introduction of the predictive maintenance system) was the "obvious" culprit.

This is also an example of how combining a "good thing" (the new and effective predictive maintenance system) with a "bad thing" (the existing *non*-C4U-compliant maintenance specs) can result in an even worse problem than before. This is because life (and everything in it) is *nonlinear* – while we humans typically visualize life (and everything in it) as being *linear*. (As we'll discuss in forthcoming chapters, *in the real world* one plus one is not necessarily two, nor is the whole always the sum of its parts, and – in fact – there actually isn't any such thing as a straight line.)

Decision Types

Once the decision-maker has been made aware of a situation requiring a decision, and has listed (or been provided a list of) the alternatives available, he or she is faced with three fundamental decision types. These are:

- *Choose* (e.g., select from among a number of alternatives ... including "do nothing")
- *Configure* (e.g., organize, construct, design a plan of action)
- *Control* (e.g., manage, regulate, govern, influence the plan of action)

Consider, for example, the decision types involved in the following situations:

- An individual has decided to invest a portion of his retirement savings in certificates of deposit (CDs). His broker has presented him with a list of CDs along with their return (interest on principal) and durations (e.g., 6 months, one year, two years, etc.). The decisions faced are:
    * Choose from among the list of CDs
    * Configure the portfolio of CDs chosen
    * Control (i.e., reinvest the maturing CDs)
- A radar system has detected an incoming object. Its radar signature has been determined. The decisions faced are:
    * *Choose* from among the possible target possibilities (e.g., hostile, friendly, non-threatening, false alarm)
    * If target is threatening, *configure* the initial launch and trajectory parameters of the intercept missile (e.g., antiballistic missile)
    * Once the intercept missile has been launched, monitor and adjust (i.e., *control*) its flight to the target
- A factory manager has been made aware of serious problems in her factory. The time required to process the typical job through the plant is excessive. She might decide to:
    * *Choose* from among the most recent sure-fire, quick-and-easy management fads

* Have "her people" implement (*configure*) and manage (*control*) the steps of the fad

Hopefully, once the factory manager in the last example reads this book she, and/or her advisors, will determine a more cost-effective and sustainable approach to decision-making. To do this, *The Three Obstacles* must be identified and surmounted.

A Brief Introduction To The Three Obstacles

The purpose of this book is to provide the reader with the ability to *recognize each of The Three Obstacles*, *identify their causes*, and to either *eliminate or – at the least – mitigate their impact*. I'll also discuss the particularly important and powerful matter of how to actually exploit those obstacles – i.e., develop strategies and tactics that enable you to employ *The Three Obstacles* to *your* advantage.

This will all be covered and illustrated in the chapters that follow. It's time, however, to briefly introduce *The Three Obstacles*, i.e., the hurdles that must be cleared if there is to be any hope of the achievement of your goals. They are:

- *Unnecessary* Complexity,
- *Excessive* Variability, and
- *Intellectual Myopia*

Notice the words in italics. Complexity in itself, for example, is not necessarily an obstacle to success; it may actually be required to achieve a given goal. It becomes an obstacle only when the complexity is *unnecessary*. The same argument holds for variability. Variability often cannot be avoided (e.g., the inherent variability of a machine ... even a so-called precision machine, or the variability of weather, or the changes in consumer preferences). Variability becomes an obstacle only when it is *excessive*.

The third obstacle, often the most frustrating, is that of *Intellectual Myopia*. Myopia is defined, when referring to the human eye, as a condition in which "our vision of distant objects is defective." It is also defined as "a lack of foresight or discernment, holding a narrow view of something, a lack of imagination or intellectual insight." Any and all of these definitions apply to *Intellectual Myopia*. In somewhat less polite terms, it could be defined as "lousy leadership" (as well as unfettered zealotry in defense of the *status quo*).

A key to success is one's ability to recognize the existence of these three obstacles. In other words, we *must* "know the enemy." If not, there is little if any hope of isolating and then overcoming the three primary obstacles to the achievement of your goal – *no matter how many fads and fashions you chase or how many motivational speakers you invite.*

My goal, in writing this book, is to provide its readers with a knowledge and understanding of the three primary obstacles to success and thus vastly improve the ability to achieve their goal (or goals) when making nontrivial decisions.

My mission is to present the readers, i.e., anyone who is truly serious about decision-making and the achievement of success (however that might be measured), with a scientifically based approach – and to do so *without the necessity to employ the scientific jargon and esoteric mathematics common to academic publications.*

This book has been written for either decision-makers, or those individuals who advise decision-makers, or the reader who simply wishes to have a better understanding of the obstacles faced by decision-makers. The book addresses the matters of how to improve decision-making, identify one's strengths and weakness, and how to improve the probability of achieving success in terms of the accomplishment of one's goals. It also serves to provide an explanation, as shall be discussed, as to the primary reason for the high failure and disappointment rate of management fads and fashions.

If you happen to be looking for a quick-and-easy "magic bullet" – an effortless way in which to achieve success in your decision-making without even having to think about it – try looking under "**M**" (for either **M**agic or **M**anagement gurus). If, however, you are seriously interested in an effective, scientifically sound and holistic method for dealing with the three primary obstacles to success (and even exploiting them), read on. On the other hand, if you are unable to tolerate any criticism – no matter how constructive or valid – of the *status quo*, or of some particular management fad, you just may have purchased the wrong book.

2. Indecision, Decisions, And Analogies

*The reason that 'guru' is such a popular word
is because 'charlatan' is so hard to spell.*
- William J. Bernstein

The squirrel (I believe his name was Marvin), his tiny heart racing and his even tinier brain in a state of utter panic, scurried forward a few squirrel paces – and then raced backwards almost precisely the same distance ... desperate, frantic moves that only served to leave him in the path of the oncoming SUV, a shiny new black Cadillac Escalade ESV mounted on 22 inch 7-spoke premium painted wheels with chrome inserts. Walter, the driver of the approaching vehicle, blissfully unaware of the furry little animal's dilemma, used his vehicle's fully integrated state-of-the-art artificially intelligent voice recognition system to change the satellite radio station, took a sip of his $37.00 cup of responsibly grown, climate-friendly, and fair-traded coconut mocha almond milk Capofredo – with four extra shots of espresso – and sped on. A split second later, little Marvin's hope of escape from his predicament was, shall we say, *squashed*.

<<<<>>>>

At roughly the same time as Marvin's untimely and

untidy demise, Major General William Tecumseh Forsyth III signed an approval form. The inclusion of the proposed fix should, the general hoped, alleviate the annoying problems that had been experienced with the pilot's helmet – a crucial part of the new, massively expensive (the $130 million, *or more*, per copy) aircraft being tested. Test pilots had complained that the half-million-dollar custom-made helmet – designed to provide the pilot with a 360-degree view outside the plane – made it difficult to move their heads inside the aircraft's cramped cockpit. The problematic helmet, along with a lengthy list of other complaints, had – an indignant pilot claimed – led to being substantially outperformed in a mock aerial dogfight against a far less advanced *40-year old* ($19 million per copy) aircraft.

<<<<>>>>

Donna Garcia, plant manager of a multi-billion-dollar semiconductor fabrication facility (aka, a "fab"), listened – impatiently – as her staff listed the massive and growing number of problems encountered in the implementation of what had been promised – by a world renowned and exceptionally well compensated management guru – to be the "latest, greatest, and most powerful methodology ever developed for the enhancement of factory performance." (*Even more powerful*, he had claimed, than his three previous "latest, greatest, and most powerful methodologies for the enhancement of factory performance.)

After hearing her staff's litany of complaints, Donna reluctantly agreed that it was time to find another approach. Picking up a copy of the most recent issue of *CEO for the 21st Century ... and Beyond*, the most respected of the numerous management newsletters she subscribed to, Donna pointed to its headline: "*Factory Assessment and Determination System: The Ultimate Solution to Production Line Performance.*"

The article cited claims of the amazing results allegedly achieved by the new, brilliant, all-powerful, and – of course – quick-and-easy *Factory Assessment and Determination System*, more commonly known as FADs. Having lost faith in the results achieved by a lengthy list of other schemes that had been tried (most of whose names and acronyms were no longer remembered), it was unanimously agreed that the fab needed, as soon as possible, to adopt FADs.

Later that day an order was placed for several thousands of T-shirts, each imprinted with the firm's logo on the front and the slogan, *FADs Rule!*, on the back. Donna Garcia slept easy that night.

<<<<>>>>

Margaret McIntyre strolled the aisles of the bookstore. The books on dieting seemed to take up at least a third of the store's massive floor space. Margaret had just given up her attempt to lose weight via a no-carb diet – the most recent of a host of other failed attempts to lose weight, including: all-carb diet, low-fat diet, vegan diet, vegetarian diet, fruitarian diet, cave-man diet, tapeworm egg diet, intermittent fasting, cookie diet, raw food diet, KE-diet, cabbage soup diet, grapefruit diet, breatharian diet [you are, no kidding, limited to inhaling air], and the Alcohol diet [far and away this author's personal favorite].

Despite the fact that her home's bookshelves were already stuffed to overflowing with diet books, Margaret was searching, yet again, for yet another diet plan. Almost all the diets she had tried had led to some weight loss ... followed soon afterwards with a return to her previous weight, if not more. Surely, she thought, there has to be some diet that will work for her — something simple, quick, easy, and ... hopefully ... tasty. Suddenly Margaret stopped in her tracks: sitting prominently on the "Latest Releases" table was a book titled: *The Deep-Fried Cricket Diet: Your Quick and Crunchy Answer to Weight Loss ... and Climate Change.*

<<<<>>>>

The massive and ever-increasing number of diet books is only matched — if not surpassed — by the massive and ever-increasing number of business/management/self-help books: books that present purportedly sure-fire, quick-and-easy ways to achieve "success." The list of such books seems to go on forever, despite the fact that few if any of their quick-and-easy schemes achieve lasting results. Instead, like the results of Margaret's diets, the situation soon returns to the norm, if not worse.

I argue that the primary reason for a lack of success, in either diet or management/self-help fads and fashions, is their failure to address *The Three Obstacles*. Consider, as but one example, the concept of "Lean," as in "Lean Manufacturing," or "Lean Thinking," or "Lean Leadership," or "Lean Healthcare," etc. Henry Ford was able to capture the essence of Lean (decades before the term was popularized) when he said: "We will not put into our establishment anything that is useless." (The only way to improve on Ford's declaration would be, in my opinion, to add the phrase "or anybody" after the word "anything.")

Most management scientists of the late 19th and early 20th centuries were focused on the elimination of waste (e.g., anything that is useless ... like CSPAN or the Kardashians). Many of their century-old ideas and developments (e.g., "value stream mapping") have been reinvented and renamed (and erroneously credited to the Japanese, or Toyota) since then. And, while reducing waste is certainly a worthy goal, it only addresses, in small part, one of *The Three Obstacles*, and – even then – only obliquely.

The four scenarios presented earlier in this chapter have two things in common. They are fictionalized representations of *actual, real-life* events and each embodies an instance in which the "decision-maker" was faced with *The Three Obstacles*. Marvin, the squirrel, incurred the fatal consequences of failing to identify and overcome those obstacles. But then, poor little Marvin was a just a squirrel with a brain the size of a jellybean.

Hopefully, the fictional General Forsyth III, an intelligent, superbly trained, and highly motivated human being, will succeed in his efforts as they could well determine the ability to defend our nation. Hopefully, the actual aircraft in question (the F-35 Lightning) will ultimately surmount its problems. Godspeed, General Forsyth.

And then there's Donna Garcia, the beleaguered semiconductor fab manager. While we wish her the best of luck, perhaps she and her staff might give some serious thought as to the rather ominous acronym (FADs) employed by this latest, greatest, final solution to production line and supply chain performance. Or to the firm's previous – and unsatisfying experience – with a host of other performance improvement schemes promising "quick-and-easy" results.

Finally, we wish Margaret McIntyre *bonne chance* in her search for a means to control her weight. Perhaps, however, she might wish to determine – with the help of her physician – the root cause of her weight problem. So, Margaret, consider putting down the tub of Chubby Hubby ice cream, tossing the super-sized bag of chocolate chip cookies, turning off the television, dusting off the exercise bicycle and, for heaven's sake, give Dr. White a call.

Keep those four vignettes in mind as you continue reading this book and its introduction to the means necessary to overcome the three primary obstacles to success. Let us move on, however, to two even more pertinent examples.

Success Achieved, Success Denied

Our success, or failure, in achieving a goal will be determined in large part by our recognition, appreciation, and understanding of the three obstacles. This may be illustrated by two more real life examples – using actual names this time – in which *The Three Obstacles* were encountered and, at least in one instance, overcome.

<<<<>>>>

Montclair, New Jersey – 1915: Frank, after loosening his tie, pored over the results of his most recent investigation. The still photos and movies that had been taken that month were of actual surgical operations, in actual hospital operating rooms. A significant difference from the typical operating room, however, was that the surgeons, nurses, and anesthesiologists that had been captured on film were all wearing numbers on their caps. Another difference was that the surfaces of the room were covered with gridded lines.

Despite the objections of some physicians, Frank (i.e., Frank Bunker Gilbreth) had been permitted by hospital administrators to take photos and movies in their operating rooms. The objective was to achieve a higher level of success *in terms of a greater number of patients surviving surgery*. A primary cause of the death (or mental or physical impairment) of surgical patients was (and still is) that of the length of the surgery. The longer the surgery takes, the greater the physical stress on the patient and, in this particular case, the greater the probability of the potentially deadly impact of the anesthetic of the day: *ether*. (The dose of ether that produces death in 50 percent of the population is only slightly higher than the dose of ether required to "reduce consciousness sufficiently.")

Frank Gilbreth, although not a physician (he began work, at age 17, as a bricklayer and never received a university degree), was a keen and practiced *observer* – an observer who was, particularly during the first two or three decades of the 20th century, renowned for his ability to vastly improve the effectiveness and efficiency of processes found in an astonishing number of seemingly very different scenarios. Gilbreth's observations of operations in hospitals led him to propose what was then a very different, very radical approach to surgery (i.e., as in the case of the message of this book, it defied conventional wisdom and gravely offended those zealously defending the *status quo*).

Gilbreth noticed that the surgeon, when changing from one surgical tool to another, had to cease focusing on the patient and, instead, look for – and then reach for – the next implement required in the performance of the procedure. As a consequence of that observation, one of several recommendations Gilbreth made was to assign one of the operating room nurses to what he termed the role of "nurse-caddy." The role of the "caddy" was to hand the next instrument, as required in the procedure, to the surgeon and remove the implement used in the previous step – a role very much *analogous* to the function of a caddy in golf.

In addition to adding a "nurse-caddy," Gilbreth also incorporated a "callback routine." For example, when the surgeon – eyes fixed on the patient – says "scalpel," the nurse-caddy will answer with "scalpel" and then hand that particular tool to the surgeon. This callback – the repeat of a verbal request – provides the surgeon with the opportunity to correct himself if he happened to have asked for the wrong implement.

The adoption of Gilbreth's nurse-caddy/callback recommendation served to significantly reduce the amount of time that a patient was sedated – and thus vastly improved his or her chances of survival. It also permitted the surgeon to more effectively focus on his primary purpose – that of conducting surgery. And it certainly made the operating rooms in television shows (e.g., *General Hospital*, *Casualty*, *Doctors*, *Emergency*, *Mash*) more entertaining.

What Gilbreth achieved was the removal or, at the very least, mitigation of the three primary obstacles to success. Nearly a century later, certain contractors to the U.S. Air Force would implement Gilbreth's recommendations in the area of aircraft maintenance, using what was sometimes termed the "nurse-surgeon-patient" approach to maintenance (i.e., one maintenance technician – the "nurse-caddy" – was charged with handing the lead technician the specific tool necessary to perform the next step in the maintenance procedure, a step read off by a third technician). The "patient," in this case, was either an aircraft or a component of the aircraft to be maintained.

While the "nurse-surgeon-patient" approach achieved significant improvement in aircraft maintenance performance, it evidently hasn't as yet received nearly the degree of adoption that it deserves – and that unnerving impediment is, as we shall see, yet another example of one of *The Three Obstacles* (*Intellectual Myopia*).

<<<<>>>>

Akron, Ohio – circa 1930: Paul, a 19-year-old Sicilian immigrant, was a regular visitor to Akron's public library. His primary reading interest, oddly enough, was that of construction – particularly construction employing stone masonry and bricklaying. Then again, perhaps that wasn't so odd. After all, Paul's father, grandfather, and great-grandfather had been stonemasons in Sicily.

Paul was, in 1930, an apprentice bricklayer and curious to learn if anyone had written anything on the art as well as the science of that ancient and honorable profession. He wanted to do more than simply stack bricks and mortar on top of other layers of bricks and mortar. In addition, Paul wanted, very much, to win a forthcoming bricklaying contest held for apprentices.

It was at the library that he happened upon a book titled: *Bricklaying System*, published in 1909 ... 21 years earlier. The author of the book claimed to have developed a system for bricklaying that increased the average number of bricks laid per hour from 125 to 350. Equally impressive, its author asserted that a bricklayer using his method could return home each night considerably less fatigued than the worker who, using conventional methods, only laid an average of 125 per hour. This apparent miracle was achieved by reducing the number of motions required per brick from 18 to 5 – in part by means of a revised workplace layout so as to reduce, for example, the number of times the bricklayer had to bend over to pick up a brick, and then stoop down once more to pick up the mortar necessary to set the brick.

Paul realized that some of what the author of *Bricklaying System* had developed to increase the number of bricks laid could not be realized in the forthcoming contest (e.g., the use of the adjustable scaffold that the book's author had invented). He was, however, able to incorporate some of the time saving techniques outlined in the book and, with the help of a younger brother (acting as a laborer), practiced the revolutionary methods in the backyard of his parent's home.

It wasn't long before it came naturally. Paul became a virtual "bricklaying machine."

Paul entered the apprentices' bricklaying contest that summer and won handily, beating his nearest competitor by almost twice the number of bricks laid. That win, however, almost cost him his apprenticeship and an end to his dream of becoming a journeyman bricklayer.

The techniques that Paul had taught himself from the bricklaying system book, were – he was informed – *too effective*. Even though the quality of his work was deemed exceptional, the bricklayer union officials attending the contest said he was *too fast*. Instead of being praised for his win, he was ordered to slow down – after all, bricklayers were paid by the hour, not by the number of bricks laid (and, of course, union dues were – and are – a function of the number of bricklayers working and paying dues, not necessarily on how fast they work).

Paul Ignizio, later to become my father, acquiesced. He had met and been defeated by what is often the most frustrating of *The Three Obstacles*. He spent the next four decades laying bricks the inefficient, physically arduous, way: The union way.

> *Bricklaying may be traced back at least 6,000 years. During that period it is estimated that the average number of bricks laid per hour had been 125. Frank Gilbreth formed a construction company in the latter part of the 19th century and his bricklayers, using the methods he developed* [Gilbreth, F. B. (1909)], *achieved a bricklaying rate of roughly 350 bricks an hour. (Gilbreth applied his methods for the removal of unnecessary motions to all facets of construction and one of his firm's most impressive achievement was the construction – in just 60 working days – of the Augustus Lowell Laboratory of Electrical Engineering at the Massachusetts Institute of Technology.)*
>
> *So, you may ask, what is the average rate of bricks laid per hour today? A few years ago the bricklayers' union in Britain demanded the establishment of a maximum average rate of 80 bricks an hour – about one fourth of that achieved by Gilbreth a*

century ago. Based on recent observations, it would appear that a rate of between 75 and 100 bricks per hour is now typical in the States. Welcome to the year 4,000 B.C.

By the way, it is important to recognize that a "good decision" today is often more beneficial than a "better, or even perfect decision" tomorrow. General George S. Patton put it this way: "A good solution applied with vigor now is better than a perfect solution applied ten minutes later." In other words, we should normally seek to overcome, eliminate, or mitigate *The Three Obstacles* as soon as possible. Or, as another general – General George Armstrong Custer – said at the battle of Little Bighorn, seconds before being shot dead, "perhaps we *should* have brought our Gatling guns." (Okay, he may have not actually said that, but I'm betting he gave it some serious thought.)

Analogies

Each of two case studies discussed previously (i.e., the nurse-caddy concept and my father's experience as an apprentice bricklayer) involved, *implicitly*, overcoming one or more of *The Three Obstacles*. While a straightforward, detailed procedure for the identification, mitigation, and exploitation of those obstacles will be presented in forthcoming chapters, it is important to note that one other important notion was also *implicitly* introduced. This is the employment of *analogies* in either making decisions or the solution of problems. An appreciation of *analogies*, in conjunction with that of *The Three Obstacles*, provides the framework for the *identification, mitigation, and even the exploitation of the primary obstacles to success* in virtually any situation.

> *One of the most well-known examples of analogies is that of the invention of Velcro. George de Mestral noticed, following a hike in 1940, the remarkable ability of cockleburs to attach themselves to his clothing and his dog's fur. Drawing upon that experience, he ultimately invented an analogous artificial device: Velcro.*

Frank Gilbreth employed, likely subconsciously, analogies in his development of his radical new solutions to the hospital operating room and bricklaying problems. He extended those analogies to numerous other seemingly – at least on the surface – different matters; e.g., the rapid assembly and disassembly of rifles and machine guns – a system still in use today. Gilbreth, as the practitioners of Lean Manufacturing attempt to accomplish today, determined where waste (e.g., in terms of wasteful motions) was and then attacked the problem by means of removing that waste (e.g., either removing a wasteful step, or replacing that step with one that provided an improvement, or even inventing a device to enable his concept). We can also employ analogies to illustrate the notions of *Unnecessary* Complexity, *Excessive* Variability, and *Intellectual Myopia*.

The Three Obstacles And Their Analogies

Analogies, if properly chosen, can be an effective way in which to illustrate a variety of concepts and notions, including *Unnecessary* Complexity, *Excessive* Variability, and *Intellectual Myopia*; i.e., *The Three Obstacles*. For example, we might wish to explain the notion of complexity ... and, in particular, *Unnecessary* Complexity.

To do so, we could use – *as an analogy* – the Heads-Up-Displays (HUDs) found in most commercial and military aircraft, or – more specifically – the simpler and more limited HUDs existing in today's automobiles (at least in the most expensive vehicles or offered as pricey options on the highest trim models).

In automobiles, HUDs consist of images (in the form of icons, graphs, gauges, numbers, etc.) that are projected onto the driver's side windshield. While they are projected on the windshield, they appear (to the driver) to be located in his or her field of vision and about two or three yards distant. As a consequence, the driver is able to see, simultaneously, both the road ahead and the display. In most vehicle HUDs the presentation will consist of such information, or their subsets, as:

- Vehicle speed
- Engine RPM
- Signs detected by a traffic sign recognition system
- Speed limits
- Lane departure warnings
- Distance from the vehicle ahead
- Next upcoming turn, or even turn-by-turn navigation
- AWD power distribution
- Compass heading
- Fuel consumption and efficiency

While heads-up-displays are assumed to be a "good thing," research has shown that they can and do lead to distracted driving. It wouldn't be hard, for example, to project *too much* information on the windshield. Imagine, for example, a HUD that presented, simultaneously, all of the previous list of information as well as:

- Radio station being listened to and its volume
- Time of day
- Oil life remaining
- Radiator fluid temperature
- Distance to next service station, restaurant, motel, roadside attraction, etc.
- Outside temperature, interior temperature, wind strength and direction
- Notification of an incoming email or text message
- Reminder of an upcoming appointment
- Etc., etc.

If "too much information" is projected on the windshield, the driver will experience what has been termed as either "data overload" or "information overload." Data, or information, overload is defined as:

> *Information overload occurs when the amount of input to a system exceeds its processing capacity. Decision makers have fairly limited cognitive processing capacity. Consequently, when information overload occurs, it is likely that a reduction in decision quality will occur*
> [Speir, C. et al. (1999)].

In other words (and in plain English), there is a point at which "too much information" is overwhelming, leading to "decision paralysis," or – if you will – a "degradation in the decisions made."

> *There are even claims that the relentless cascade of information lowers people's intelligence. A few years ago, a study commissioned by Hewlett-Packard reported that the IQ scores of knowledge workers distracted by e-mail and phone calls fell from their normal level by an average of 10 points – twice the decline for those smoking marijuana ...* [Hemp, P. (2009].

Before the reader becomes distracted by the simultaneous mention of marijuana and the surname of the author (i.e., *Hemp*) in the referenced article, I'll return to the analogy between HUDs and *complexity*. The windshield projection of a HUD represents, if the number of individual data displays are "large," *complexity*. If that number can be reduced without degradation to the driver's performance (or if the reduction actually provides an improvement), then the original display was *unnecessarily* complex.

Next, consider an analogy for *variability*. If the individual elements of the HUD were to, for example, randomly change places (e.g., the RPM icon changes places with the outside temperature icon), or randomly takes on a different shape or form, we would be experiencing *variability*. And, if the frequency and number of random exchanges are so "large" as to degrade driver performance, we would be experiencing *Excessive* Variability.

In other words, if a decision to include a HUD on an automobile is based on the desire to improve driver performance, it should factor in – and attempt to overcome – the first two obstacles (i.e., *Unnecessary* Complexity and *Excessive* Variability). It might be noted that the number one complaint of new car buyers, according to a 2016 *J.D. Powers* report, is that of problems (e.g., difficulty of use) with their advanced technology.

The HUD analogy to the third obstacle, *Intellectual Myopia*, would be evident if the senior management of car manufacturers continued to fail to take the complaints of vehicle owners, with regard to HUD or any other "advanced automotive technology" seriously.

<<<<>>>>

There is yet another analogy that should be mentioned. The physical property known as "friction" serves as a resistance to physical movement. The Three Obstacles are, in fact, analogous to friction in that they also serve as a type of resistance – specifically, an impediment to success. Furthermore, just as there are ways in which to overcome friction (e.g., the invention of the wheel and axle), and even exploit friction (e.g., the brake), there are ways in which to overcome and even exploit *The Three Obstacles*.

Chapter Summary

The Three Obstacles impose an obstruction – whether we recognize it or not – to the solution of virtually every nontrivial problem we encounter. *The degree of success – or failure – we achieve is dependent upon our ability to identify those obstacles and remove, avoid, or at the very least, mitigate their impact.* Frank Gilbreth recognized that an increase in the number of bricks laid an hour could be achieved via the reduction of *unnecessary motions*. He employed an analogous approach to the reduction of unnecessary motions in the operating room, as well as in the assembly and disassembly of small firearms – and numerous other scenarios.

While Gilbreth focused on the reduction of unnecessary motions (e.g., one type of *Unnecessary* Complexity) to improve procedures, there are a host of other *unnecessary factors* that serve to impede and degrade the decisions we make. Reduction of "the unnecessary" (e.g., motions, process steps, rules, laws, alternatives, layers, parts, almost all faculty meetings, certain team members, adherence to traditions, certain required courses in university, most PowerPoint presentations, most video games, etc.) plays a key role in the achievement of success, however it might be measured. The "trick" is to determine just what is unnecessary, and what is necessary, and then respond accordingly. In the next chapter, the first obstacle to success, *Unnecessary* Complexity, is addressed in detail. As we shall see, wasteful motions are but one example of *Unnecessary* Complexity.

3. Unnecessary Complexity

Simplicity is the ultimate sophistication.
— Leonardo da Vinci

Truth is ever to be found in simplicity, and not in the multiplicity and confusion of things.
— Isaac Newton

As cited in the quotes directly above, Leonardo da Vinci and Isaac Newton – not exactly slouches in problem solving – recognized, centuries ago, the critical importance of simplicity. Blissfully ignorant of their sage advice, I graduated college indoctrinated in the belief "that which was new" and "that which reflected the latest, greatest advances in science" was the only rational solution to virtually any decision. To think otherwise, I had been taught, was to be primitive, unlearned, backward, ignorant, and just plain foolish. In fact, one of my professors had said that we (i.e., his students) had a choice: either remain ignorant Luddites or accept the indisputable fact that "new is always better."

That naïve belief, and that indoctrination, played a role – thankfully only briefly – in my first job after graduating college. In 1962 I was hired by the North American Aviation Company (aka, NAA). NAA had received contracts from the government to analyze, design, build, test, prepare, and support the launch of the second stage of the launch vehicle for the Saturn V/Apollo manned moon-landing mission, as well as the Apollo capsule itself. As a freshly minted electrical engineering graduate, I was delighted to be even a small part of that heroic, ambitious effort to place American astronauts on the moon (and, of course, beat the Soviet Union – the Russians – to that lofty destination).

Some months after joining the firm, I attended a meeting at which Dr. Wernher von Braun, Director of the Marshall Space Flight Center and "father of the Saturn V" (as well at the "father" of the V2 rockets that rained down death and destruction on Britain during WW2), was to speak. He was to give a presentation on the essential role that the Saturn V launch vehicle (i.e., the three stages consisting of the S-IC, S-II, and S-IVB) was to play in the Apollo program. Despite being assigned a seat in the very last row of the auditorium, I was thrilled to have been given the opportunity to listen to von Braun.

My spirits soared as von Braun spoke of our mission, the vital importance of a manned landing on the moon, and even the eventual manned landing (scheduled, if I recall correctly, for 1986) on the planet Mars. To a greenhorn from the Midwest (aka, flyover country, the sticks, the boondocks, Hicksville, or Nowheresville), this was indeed the stuff of dreams. And I was to be a part of it!

Within a few months of my hire I was promoted to the position of lead engineer of the S-II RF (radio frequency) group. As one part of that assignment, I was tasked to determine (i) the number and type of antennas on the second stage (and their supporting components), (ii) where to deploy the antennas about the circumference of the S-II so as to maximize the probability that their signals would be received (and transmitted), no matter the inflight position of the S-II, (iii) how to test the antennas and their components so as to validate their performance, and – ultimately (iv) how to best monitor them on the launch pad and in flight.

Much like certain people today (and you know who you are), who would rather die of embarrassment then be seen with a flip-phone from the 90s and can't conceive of owning anything other than very latest smartphone (in the very latest color, with the largest screen and newest, highest resolution front and back cameras), I was keen on recommending the very latest, state-of-the-art antenna system. Specifically, I wanted the S-II, on its historic flights in support of landing men on the moon, to employ an *adaptive phased array antenna system*. Even the very phrase, *adaptive phased array antenna system*, set my heart racing.

That dream was, however, shattered when I was informed that the Apollo mission would rely on launch vehicles that employed, *whenever, and wherever possible*, tried, true, and thoroughly tested components. Unfortunately, adaptive phased array antenna systems were not, at that time, tried, true, nor thoroughly tested. In fact, even today they remain a complex, delicate system.

I had to give up any hope of a "sophisticated state-of-the-art antenna system" and, instead, developed a static array of "simple," flush mounted, slot antennas. Despite the "primitive" and unexciting nature of that design, the performance of the S-II's antenna system in the launches of the Apollo was exemplary. (As my grandfather once told me, you can do an awful lot with just a Swiss Army Knife.)

At that early point in my now more than half-century career, I must admit to having been disappointed that I hadn't been able to equip the S-II with a more "advanced and complex" system. Today, I am far, far more disappointed that, not only can't our astronauts any longer reach the moon, we have to call a Russian "taxi" (at the cost of $82 million or more per seat) just to transport our astronauts to the International Space Station (the ISS is in orbit just 249 miles above the earth's surface, rather than the roughly 240,000 miles required to travel to the moon).

The one thing you can say, however, about today's launch vehicles is that they are most definitely far, far more complex than those old, tried and true boosters we so successfully employed a half-century ago ... those old-fashioned, embarrassingly simple, liquid-fueled rockets we used to support the program that successfully placed our astronauts on the moon.

And yes, I am being sarcastic. And bitter.

As I write this, nearly 50 years after the first manned landing on the moon, the Saturn V remains the tallest, heaviest, and most powerful rocket ever brought to operational status: and the most successful, by any measure. While it was certainly complex, the avoidance of *Unnecessary* Complexity was, I am absolutely convinced, a significant reason for its success.

There are, however, some people who worship at the altar of complexity ... even *Unnecessary* Complexity. I've certainly met an awful lot of them.

The Yo-Yo Effect

Some years ago I was invited, by the plant manager of a recently constructed semiconductor fab (i.e., a microelectronics factory in which integrated circuits – "computer chips" – were manufactured), to visit his recently constructed factory and recommend ways in which to improve its performance. I sensed a hint of desperation in his voice (a signal, by the way, that can draw management consultants like bees to honey ... or like vultures to road kill).

Upon arriving at his office, I was informed that the manager was running late. His administrative assistant invited me to wait in one of the exceptionally comfortable, padded, soft Corinthian leather chairs in the manager's office.

Still suffering somewhat from the effects of jetlag, I took a seat in the plant manager's office and was about to "rest my eyes" when I noticed two large, well-stocked, bookcases. Curious as to just what the manager might be reading, I scanned the titles on the spines of the books. They were, almost without exception, books on various approaches to the improvement of the operation of factories, production lines, and supply chains, or those claiming to enhance one's effectiveness as a leader. The topics ranged from ways to encourage teamwork, become a more successful/influential executive, and identifying one's strengths, to concepts addressing somewhat more quantifiable topics for the enhancement of production line performance (e.g., total quality management, reengineering, quality circles, theory of constraints, lean manufacturing, value streams, six sigma, etc.).

Those bookcases, and the large number of books

advocating a vast array of alleged solutions to a manager's problems (coupled with the complete and total absence of books on *the history* of management, manufacturing, or manufacturing science), set off alarm bells. It has been my experience to find that, the more books on improvement/enhancement schemes on a manager's shelves, the less likely it is that he or she will make and follow the decisions that lead to significant and – particularly – sustainable improvement in factory (or supply chain, business process, etc.) performance. In fact, the more books they have on management and manufacturing fads, the more they seem to continue to flail about in a frantic, desperate search for a quick-and-easy solution – a "magic bullet." (Remember the story of Margaret McIntyre and her search for a diet plan?)

An acquaintance of mine, a clinical psychologist, observed the same phenomena in her appointments and house visits with morbidly obese clients. She correlated the number of books on dieting in the client's home with the likelihood of an individual ever being able to achieve a normal weight and – most important – retain that more healthy weight. In short, the relationship was inversely proportional: *The more the books* on the subject, *the less likely the success* [Ignizio, J. P. (2008)].

A few minutes later the plant manager, an intense and nervous man in his early forties, walked in. After exchanging pleasantries, he proceeded to – with considerable pride – describe various features of his fab: the features he evidently thought the most important and impressive. These included:

- The enormous size of the fab

- The truly massive number of "tools" (i.e., machines – such as photolithography, etchers, metrology, etc. – used to produce the computer chips) the fab contained
- The number of process steps (in the hundreds) required to produce each semiconductor "wafer" (the silicon surface upon which computer chips are deposited)
- The complexity of the "recipe" and the highly reentrant production path necessary to produce each wafer
- The complex, highly automated system for transporting semiconductor wafers from one processing station to another
- The (quite enormous) amount of money that had been expended to build the fab, purchase the tools, provide its inventory, and train and pay its large (and high turnover rate) labor force

After finishing his impassioned and impromptu presentation, the manager got to the point – the specific reason he had asked me to meet with him. While he had a massive, complex, expensive, state-of-the-art facility, its performance was far less than had been anticipated – or had been predicted by a costly, time consuming series of computer simulations. In fact, the facility's actual performance was quite dismal despite all the motivational speakers they had invited and all the sure-fire, quick-and-easy, performance improvement methods they had tried – and it certainly deviated significantly from the spectacular results that had been projected by means of simulation.

The plant manager wanted, quite desperately (not something, by the way, you should ever reveal to a consultant) to find a way (quick-and-easy, of course) to significantly improve his fab's performance. He was also baffled (as were his staff) as to just why the elaborate, detailed, and highly touted simulation package they had used had so badly failed to predict his fab's *actual* performance. (I'll return to that matter in a forthcoming chapter.)

Ironically, while the plant manager and his senior staff were infatuated with the massive cost and extreme complexity of the fab, they made it clear that they wanted a *cheap*, fast, quick-and-easy solution to their (serious and massive costly) problems.

Up, Up And Away

Some years ago Robert, a university professor with expertise in statistics, was asked to observe a "flight readiness evaluation" at an Air Force base in the United States. The purpose of the evaluation was to record and determine the percentage of aircraft, of a particular class, that were ready, at a given point in time, to successfully conduct a unique mission (a mission that, in the event of an attack on our country, could be critical to its defense). Robert sat in an observation tower and watched the aircraft line up on the runway and, ultimately, soar into the sky. He counted *four* aircraft taking off.

But this particular exercise was intended to evaluate the readiness of *six* aircraft. Two of the aircraft had, however, been rushed into (*unscheduled*) maintenance that very day and thus only four planes were capable of launch. In other words, only 67 percent of the aircraft involved in the test were "combat ready" – *if one limits that statistic to the aircraft that launched.*

While that sounds worrisome (i.e., only a 67 percent "readiness"), Robert was able to view another, very private, very confidential set of data. Of the four aircraft that had been launched, *two had to return to base within minutes, or even seconds, after their launch* – due to a variety of serious problems. Yet those aborted flights had been counted toward the success rate.

So, while official records showed that 67 percent of that particular fleet was "combat ready," only two of the six aircraft were able to actually accomplish their mission, a mock mission conducted under far, far less rigorous conditions than would be faced in any actual wartime situation.

In other words, while the official level of fleet readiness reported that day was a dismal 67 percent, the true measure of readiness was an even more dismal 33 percent! It wasn't any surprise to discover that the low, entirely unacceptable, readiness rate was due to *The Three Obstacles* – particularly that of *Unnecessary* Complexity in their maintenance program.

Unnecessary Complexity: A Definition

Albert Einstein said that "Everything should be made as simple as possible, but not simpler." One indication of the existence of the first obstacle to success is when the decision-maker is infatuated (as had been the fab manager in a previous vignette) with complexity. Complexity can, however, be a major obstacle to success (however success might be measured). This is true in the instances in which we ignore Einstein's advice (or that of Newton and da Vinci) and impose *Unnecessary* Complexity on a given system.

Unnecessary Complexity is the first of *The Three Obstacles* to be covered in detail (although it played a prominent role in the problems cited in previous case studies and vignettes). First, however, let's attempt to define complexity. If we look up the definition of "complexity" in dictionaries, we will probably be given a number of truly unsatisfying, frustratingly circular definitions such as (and I'm not kidding):

Complexity ... *the state of being complex*
Complexity ... *the state of not being simple*

Such absurd "definitions" are akin to defining the attribute "bad" as ... *not good*.

In 1954, United States Supreme Court Justice Potter Stewart, when the court was dealing with the notion of obscenity, said ... "I'll know it when I see it ..." That notion, however unsatisfying, is very much what we might be (if relying on a dictionary) left with in attempting to define complexity.

While complexity may be difficult to define, *Unnecessary* Complexity is – in my opinion – much easier. My personal definition of *unnecessarily complex* is:

Any system (problem, strategy, tactic, scheme, plan, design, concept) that may be made simpler while still satisfying its purpose and goals is unnecessarily complex.

Recall Frank Gilbreth's development of a bricklaying system? Gilbreth identified the unnecessary motions involved in bricklaying and either removed or simplified them. In other words, he realized that the classical method of laying bricks was, indeed, unnecessarily complex.

One man, Reuben Garrett Goldberg (better known as Rube Goldberg), made his reputation and fortune by inventing and drawing cartoons of absurdly unnecessarily complex systems ... systems that unmistakably employed unnecessary parts, superfluous operations, and farcical features in the conduct of achieving a simple task. As an example, one of Goldberg's most famous cartoons is that of "a self-operating napkin," an unnecessarily complex contrivance (a contraption involving a parrot, a cracker, a skyrocket, and cigar lighter ... among other things) designed to wipe one's face with a napkin.

While Rube Goldberg's cartoon inventions were obviously and unmistakably unnecessarily complex, it's not always as easy to recognize real life systems/strategies/tactics that are unnecessarily complex. Faced with a given "system," one way to determine if it, or its operation, is unnecessarily complex is to focus on each part, or feature, and attempt to determine if that part or feature is absolutely necessary for the achievement of the desired outcome – or if the system's performance could actually be achieved or even improved with the removal of a given part or feature, or by its replacement with a simpler, less costly item.

Another, sometimes preferable, approach is to "start from scratch." Define, succinctly, the purpose and goals of the system and then develop a less complex system, one element at the time.

> *The "start from the scratch" approach was the main thrust of a managerial fad of the 1990s: Business Process Reengineering, or BPR – a scheme in which companies start with a blank sheet of paper and rethink*

(modify or remove) existing processes so as to "deliver more value to the customer." Unfortunately, firms that adopted the concept focused their attention mainly on the reduction of their workforce by means of layoffs and outsourcing. As a consequence, firms (and government organizations) that adopted BPR *ultimately wound up even worse off than before its adoption.*

Shopping In The Soviet Union

If you either lived in or visited the Soviet Union in the 70s or 80s, you were likely witness to lots and lots of *Unnecessary* Complexity. Consider, as just one example, the steps required to purchase an item in a Soviet-era shop.

To purchase an item it was necessary to queue up *three* times. First you stood in the line established simply to permit you to gaze upon the goods. Assuming you found an item you wanted to buy, you next stood in another line to purchase, *not the item*, but the ticket necessary to buy it. Finally, you queued up in yet another line to receive the item.

In America, and most other countries at that time (and, of course, decades before shopping on the Internet), you walked into a shop, picked up the item you wished to buy, and then queued up at the cash register where you paid for the item and exited the store. In other words, instead of enduring three queues to purchase an item, you only had to deal with one (and, of course, the exasperating woman in front of you that has to search through her purse to find her readers, favorite ballpoint pen, and checkbook – but then I digress). The Soviet era shopping system clearly involved *Unnecessary* Complexity; complexity easily removed by the systems employed in capitalistic societies.

But, before you conclude that the Soviet era shopping practices were, let's say, dumb, you may want to give that matter a little more thought. *This is true whenever you run into an unnecessarily complex system.* Ask yourself this question: While the system may be unnecessarily complex, does that complexity actually benefit someone, or some group, or some organization, or some branch of government? (You may be surprised at just how many times the answer to that question is a resounding, *yes*.)

When you ask such a question of the Soviet era shopping practices, you may note that their apparent *Unnecessary* Complexity served to add more "jobs" to the economy. They may not have been necessary jobs but they did provide employment (or at least a record of "employment") to those that were given (and the key word may be "given") those unnecessary positions within a country (a "worker's paradise") that proudly claimed to have *zero* unemployment.

In short, there may be (and often is) something other than ignorance that has led to the Unnecessary Complexity. You must also realize that *complexity can be weaponized* – and in some cases *you* may be either the target or simply "collateral damage," as illustrated next (and to be discussed in detail in a forthcoming chapter).

Unnecessary Complexity And The IRS

Before we congratulate ourselves for having employed a less complex system for purchasing goods than the former Soviet Union, consider the oftentimes mind-numbing complexity involved in filing our income taxes. Just a few of the findings of the National Taxpayers Union [Brady, D. (2016); Olson, N. E. (2017)] include the following facts:

- year 2016 estimates of the time (6.1 billion hours) plus out-of-pocket costs expended annually (to file taxes) amounted to an economic loss to our nation of $234.4 billion
- in 2012 it was estimated that the tax code contained almost 4 million words
- in 1935 the 1040 form consisted of one page and two instruction pages; in 2015 the 1040 form consisted of two pages, but the number of its instruction pages had increased to 211
- to add insult to injury, the number of identity theft cases – evidently caused by the ease of hacking IRS computer systems – had risen from nearly zero in 2008 to 2.4 million in 2013

Even the average, middle-class person filling out his or her 1040 form, has surely recognized that filing an income tax form, and recording and compiling the supporting files, is frustratingly complex. But, is it *unnecessarily* complex?

One of the best-selling income tax guides is *J. K. Lasser's Your Income Tax*. In 2017, the guide was 864-pages long. Unfortunately, although the guide is helpful, just like the IRS tax code, it is still ambiguous and incomplete. If you call the IRS for assistance – and are fortunate enough to have someone answer – you'll likely discover that they (the employees tasked with answering our questions) either do not know the answer or (quite possibly worse) provide you with questionable advice.

According to a CBS News report in 2003, IRS centers established to help people prepare their tax returns gave incorrect answers – or no answer at all – to 43 percent of the questions asked by Treasury Department investigators posing as taxpayers [Cosgrove-Mather, B. (2003)]. If these (taxpayer funded) "help centers" can't provide correct answers then you know that the tax code is definitely complex. But, again, is it *unnecessarily* complex?

- Tax lawyers don't think so.
- Law schools don't think so.
- Tax preparers – particularly large firms like H&R Block, don't think so.
- Tax software suppliers certainly don't think so.
- The massive number of employees (80,000) in the IRS – and their dependents – don't think so.
- Washington's K-Street Lobbyists don't think so.
- Those congressmen and women who, mysteriously, grow enormously wealthy in their roles as public servants – and who are so effectively wooed by K-Street lobbyists – certainly don't seem to think so.
- Those "lucky" few that benefit from very special, narrowly targeted deductions, and can afford to hire the help necessary to monitor and file their taxes, absolutely don't think so.

In other words, there are matters in life that may be *unnecessarily* complex to some (e.g., the average taxpayer) while actually being *necessarily* complex to others (e.g., politicians, the mega-rich, and large companies, i.e., those who benefit from complexity). This is but one example how *Unnecessary* Complexity may be *exploited*: the topic of a forthcoming chapter. You'll see, in that chapter, just how *you* can use *Unnecessary* Complexity to *your* advantage – or, equally important, how to recognize when it is being used against you (and it definitely is).

Unnecessary Complexity And National Defense

While the *Unnecessary* Complexity of our nation's tax code may be a frustration (unless that complexity is to your benefit), *Unnecessary* Complexity in our military is an existential threat to every citizen [Lehman, J. (2017)].

John Lehman, a former secretary of the Navy, provided an overview of the impact of complexity (and *Unnecessary* Complexity) in his April 28, 2017 opinion piece in the *Wall Street Journal*. One of the examples he cites is the elapsed time from the drawing board to deployment of our nation's blue water navy ships (although this could as well be applied to our military aircraft or our air defense weapons systems as well – or even to the rebuilding of our crumbling national infrastructure).

In the late 1950s the Polaris nuclear-missile system – a massively complex system that included the nuclear submarine, solid-fuel missile, underwater launch system, nuclear warhead, and guidance system – went from drawing board to actual deployment in just four years (using, as Lehman points out, *slide rules*). Today the average development timeline *for much less complex weapon systems* is an astounding 22.5 years! (Using digital computers that seem to be constantly hacked, lost, or broken.)

Think about that; in just the past 20 years (i.e., from 1997 to 2017), the following changes or inventions in technology have happened:

- Smartphones
- Hybrid cars
- Human genome effort completed
- GPS enters civilian sector (e.g., SatNav)
- Text messaging
- Google and Facebook go public
- Amazon Kindle
- Driverless cars
- YouTube
- AbioCor artificial heart
- Skype
- and, of course, MyPillow®

If those developments occurred in just 20 years in the civilian world, think of what has happened in the military sector over the same two decades. In short, what may have been considered state-of-the-art when a weapon system was first conceived is unlikely to be nearly as revolutionary (or as effective) two or more decades later.

Before jumping to the erroneous conclusion that Lehman's article implies that "less complex systems" require a much longer time to deploy than more complex systems, it is necessary to determine just where the real complexity lies in the development and deployment of our military's weapon systems.

The answer may be summarized in one word: *Regulations*.

While the Polaris system of the 1950s was a massively complex system, it did not have to endure the ever-increasing number and type of regulations imposed on our military systems (and this holds true for a host of other "systems," including those of civilian firms, organizations, farmlands, and individuals) of today. Based upon my own experience, I seriously doubt that the Apollo manned moon-landing mission, proposed in 1961 and accomplished but eight years later, could have been achieved in even twice that time if we had been subject to the enormous number of rules, regulations, paperwork, and hours of infantile PowerPoint presentations so common today. In fact, if we had been subject to the constant, massive flow of regulations experienced today, I seriously wonder if that mission could have *ever* been achieved.

Unnecessary Complexity And Tradition

Ever been to a baseball game? Ever marveled at the *windup* of the pitcher? Conventional wisdom has said that the windup is to be used whenever there are no runners on base. If, however, there *are* runners on base then the pitcher should resort to what is called the *stretch*, supposedly a less effective procedure.

For the moment, let's assume that the pitcher happens to be right-handed. The right-handed pitcher's windup pitch consists of the following steps:

> The pitcher faces the batter, his feet pointing in the direction of home

plate.

The pitcher, his right foot on the pitching mound's rubber plate, takes a step back with his left foot.

He then turns 90 degrees to the right (he will now be facing third base).

While making that turn, he lifts his left leg, bends it at the knee, and hurls the baseball to the catcher.

The mechanics of the stretch are, however, much simpler – and require fewer motions. The steps involved in pitching from the stretch (assuming, again, a right-handed pitcher) are:

Start with both feet pointed toward third base (notice that this is the *third* step of the windup pitch).

Lift the left leg while bending at the knee.

Take a step toward home plate ... and while taking that step, hurl the baseball to the catcher.

For decades conventional wisdom held that the stretch reduced the velocity of the pitch *and* placed more strain on the pitcher's arm. Science has proven that this belief is simply not true. It is, in fact, wrong on both counts. Not only can the pitcher throw the ball just as fast as from the windup, he incurs less strain on his pitching arm. In addition, it is easier to focus on learning and practicing just one type of pitch ... that of pitching from the stretch [Diamond, J. (2017)].

To summarize, the stretch requires fewer motions – and induces less stress on a baseball pitcher, at no sacrifice to velocity. Does that sound familiar? It should be as the approach (eliminate unnecessary motions; i.e., *Unnecessary* Complexity) is *analogous* to the bricklaying system that Frank Gilbreth devised to increase the number of bricks laid each hour – with less physical stress on the bricklayer. In short, the windup is *unnecessarily* complex.

The superiority of the stretch pitch over the windup, or Gilbreth's bricklaying system over the classical approach, are but two examples of how an adherence to tradition (i.e., an unwillingness to change, or to even consider change – hallmarks of *Intellectual Myopia*) serves to inhibit the reduction of *Unnecessary* Complexity.

Walter Havisham Has His Problems

Remember Walter (i.e., Walter Prescott Havisham), the distracted driver of the SUV that squashed poor little Marvin, the squirrel? Putting aside the fact that Walter should – if there were any justice in this world – be convicted of squirrel-slaughter, consider a very serious problem he is facing at work.

Walter's company receives, reviews, and processes claim forms. Since an essential part of the decision reached (i.e., to accept, reject, or request additional information) is based on an interpretation of a written summary – *provided in free form by the claimant* – there is no way to completely automate the process.

The bottleneck (aka "constraint" or "chokepoint") in the process appears to be that of the group of employees (located in Processing Unit X) that must read and assess the written summaries and, when necessary, request additional details. Everything in the claims process appears to be going smoothly until the forms reach Unit X.

Every four hours the forms that have been processed by the group of employees immediately prior to Unit X are hand delivered to Unit X's inbox, where they wait ... and wait ... for processing. In other words, Unit X is (or appears to be) a serious bottleneck.

Walter is considering several options. He could hire and train workers to supplement those in Unit X. He could bring in efficiency experts to train the existing employees in Unit X so that they might speed up their efforts. He could offer bonuses to entice the workers in Unit X to "work faster" – which might backfire if they accept claims that have no merit (or file their own complaint as to the impact of the stress involved in the increased workload). He could even pay yet another motivational speaker to give yet another inspirational talk (e.g., perhaps on how to unlock the alleged unused 90 percent of his employees' brains).

Or Walter might want to consider a proposal by a firm (AAE, Inc. – whose motto is: "**AI** is the **A**nswer to **E**verything") that desperately wants to investigate the possibility of designing an AI (artificial intelligence) system to automate the claim's processes. (Given the firm's name, do realize that there is of course zero chance that anything other than an AI approach will be proposed.)

To add to Walter's frustration, old, cranky Fred Xavier Smith (he's worn the same, coffee stained tie for 30 years) had asked for a meeting. In that meeting, Fred presented Walter with a much simpler problem, that of determining the answer to a hypothetical "processing unit." (Fred has a particularly irritating habit of diverting Fred's attention from the real problem to some simple, silly little problem.)

The problem Fred posed was:

> *Jobs arrive at a processing station – one that simply polishes the product and sends it to a delivery station. Jobs (items to be polished) arrive, on average, every five minutes. It takes, on average, two minutes to perform the polishing operation.*

"How long, on average," Fred asked, "would it take to complete 100 jobs?"

Walter wondered how many years he would get if he strangled Fred.

"Okay," said Walter, wearily, "I'll bite. One hundred jobs arriving every five minutes, processed at two minutes per job? Well, the 99th job will arrive at 99 *times* five minutes, or 495 minutes after the first job is started, and be finished two minutes later. So it takes 495 minutes plus two minutes, or 497 minutes to finish the hundred jobs. Fred, for heaven's sake, I can add, subtract, multiply, and divide – and don't forget that I've got a Harvard MBA. By the way, it's ridiculous to have an arrival rate of every *five minutes* if it only takes *two minutes* to do the job. That's just plain wasteful. Anything else you wanted to talk about, Fred? I've really got other things I need to take care of."

"Just one more thing," said Fred, doing his very best imitation of the star of the television series: *Columbo*, "what if you sent jobs to the processing station *in batches*? Instead of a single job arriving, on average, every five minutes, what if you sent a batch of 10 jobs to the processing unit every 50 minutes on average? How long would it take to finish the 100 jobs if you used this batching scheme?"

Walter, taken aback by what he considered yet another really dumb question, performed a few calculations in his head, and then replied. "Well, the last batch of 10 jobs per batch would arrive, obviously, 450 minutes after the first. You'd complete that batch of 10 jobs, at a rate of 2 minutes a job, in 20 minutes. Add 450 minutes to 20 and you'd be finished with the hundred jobs – using batching – in 470 minutes. So, Fred, it would take 10 batches precisely 470 minutes to finish the 100 jobs. I suppose you're trying to tell me that batching will help. I'm sorry, old man, everybody knows that. That's why we're already using batching for our claim forms processing."

"No, boss," said Fred, "that's not at all what I'm saying. What I'm saying is that you're ignoring a critical factor. And that's why there's such a huge problem in the processing of our claims. Boss, you really need to look at the bigger picture."

Walter couldn't stand it any longer. "Fred, for heaven's sake, you're 71 years old. Why in the world are you worrying about these problems? Fred, you've been a loyal employee and that's why I'm making you an offer you can't refuse. Retire now and you'll receive a generous severance payout. Your only other option is to be fired. Which one is it, Fred?"

<<<<>>>>

Walter Prescott Havisham, despite his Harvard MBA and lifetime subscription to the *Harvard Business Review*, has just failed to recognize the first two obstacles to success. On the other hand, Fred Smith, the cantankerous, irritating old man who insists on speaking in parables, has just encountered the third obstacle: *Intellectual Myopia*. As a consequence, both men have failed in their attempt to achieve any degree of success in the solution to the problems in the firm's claims processing procedure. Instead, Fred has been "sent out to pasture" and Walter is likely to try one costly, ineffective, and inappropriate fad after another ... approaches that will fail to provide an efficient, cost-effective solution to the firm's problem.

<<<<>>>>

Given the information provided above, can you, reader, answer the questions asked by Fred Xavier Smith? How long will it *actually* take to complete the 100 jobs without batching? How long will it *actually* take to complete the 100 jobs if you use batching?

I'll provide you with the answers to both questions right now. **You don't know!** You *cannot* know the answers unless you have an appreciation and understanding of the first and second obstacles to success and an appreciation and understanding of the causes of those impediments. I'll leave it to a later chapter to provide a more detailed explanation. For now, just remember that *one plus one is not necessarily two* (and its corollary: *the whole is not necessarily equal to the sum of its parts*. Seriously.).

The Crucial Importance Of Observation

Rather than rushing into a situation and attempting to solve it by some allegedly sure-fire, quick-and-easy, never-fail scheme, it's vital to take the time necessary to thoroughly understand the problem ... and the decision-maker's goal. This can only be accomplished if you take the time and effort necessary to observe. Then, if your focus is on the reduction of *Unnecessary* Complexity, you might take a lesson from Frank Bunker Gilbreth, author of the *Bricklaying System* book.

Before Gilbreth attempted to delete or modify anything he might have thought to be unnecessarily complex, he took the time to closely *observe the system in question* (e.g., the operating room surgeon). Equally important, he did not restrict his attention to just the surgeon (i.e., to just one aspect of the problem). Instead, he viewed the entire operating room, all of its personnel, the surgical procedure, and the instruments employed. He also took the time and effort to gain some appreciation as to the "why and how" of surgical operations. *Frank Gilbreth focused his attention on the whole system rather than on just the portion of the system in which, according to conventional wisdom, the problem supposedly existed.*

In short, the first step involved in the removal of waste in the form of *Unnecessary* Complexity is to become familiar with the existing procedures – and, when possible, their *raison d'être*. There is absolutely no substitute for observation.

*It is important to realize that a fundamental part of "observation" is that of obtaining, whenever possible, an appreciation of the **history** of the problem. Not only might this provide you with a better understanding of the situation, it may help avoid repeating the mistakes of the past.*

Rather than rushing into a situation, with the latest, greatest, sure-fire scheme, first take the time to thoroughly understand the problem, its goal(s), environment, purpose, and constraints. Discuss, if feasible, the problem with the personnel most familiar with the situation. Try to determine what actions may have previously been taken in an attempt to resolve the problem (i.e., it just might be that the problem faced has been caused or exacerbated by actions – including the adoption of fads – taken in the past).

Once those preliminary steps have been accomplished, consider just how the process might be simplified (i.e., made less complex, if that is indeed the problem) while still achieving its purpose.

Then, before rushing to implement your findings, consult the firm or organization's experts once again – those responsible for oversight of the existing procedures. They will likely point out real – as well as imagined – problems with your proposal. You may, in fact, be facing – at that time – the most dreaded of all obstacles: *Intellectual Myopia.*

Before proceeding further, realize that while I've provided some illustrations of *Unnecessary* Complexity, and advice on its reduction, I haven't as yet talked about how it might, in certain instances, *be measured*, and done so objectively. That extremely important matter will be discussed in a following chapter. First, however, consider another one of Fred Xavier Smith's "silly little problems."

Assume that you drive a car uphill for 100 miles at a miles-per gallon consumption rate of precisely one (i.e., one mile per gallon). Then you drive it downhill for another 100 miles, at a rate of 100 mpg. What, Fred asks, is your average mpg rate for that 200-mile trip, i.e., is it approximately (i.e., *rounded off to the nearest integer*):

a. 25 mpg

b. 50 mpg

c. 2 mpg

d. or none of the above?

Before you answer, make sure that you have not:

(i) simply reacted, impulsively, to the question, or (ii) overcomplicated the situation. (The answer to this question will be addressed in a chapter to follow.)

Chapter Summary

In this chapter I've presented a broad overview of *Unnecessary* Complexity. It should be clear that *Unnecessary* Complexity may be an elusive, and even subjective, concept. How do we know, for example, that what we have done to reduce complexity hasn't actually worsened the performance of the system in question, rather than improved it? What if, however, you could determine a reasonably satisfying means to *measure* complexity? How might this help us to reduce *Unnecessary* Complexity?

We'll introduce that topic in the following chapter. First, however, let's consider yet one more quote with regard to complexity.

> *Complexity is your enemy. Any fool can make something complicated. It is hard to keep things simple.* – Richard Branson

With Branson's quote in mind, you may want to give the gasoline mileage problem another try.

4. Excessive Variability

*The excessive increase in anything
causes a reaction in the opposite direction.*
— Plato

Dictionary definitions of *variability* – the subject of this chapter – include: *changeable, inconstant, fickle, lack of consistency of a fixed pattern,* and *liability to vary.* Two definitions common to the field of statistics, and more pertinent to our discussion, are: the *spread or dispersion of data,* or (in particular) *divergence from the average.* The data plots of Figures 4.1(a) and 4.1(b) represent, respectively, examples of data having little dispersion (Clustered Data, on the left) and that with considerable dispersion (Widely Dispersed Data, on the right). While both may have the same averages, their impact can be (and likely will be) significantly different.

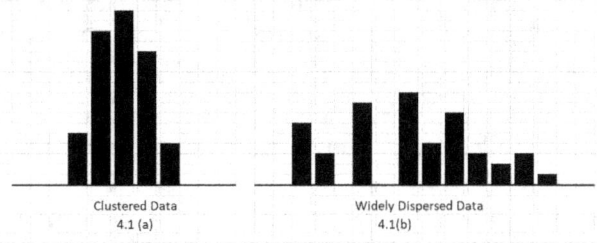

Figure 4.1

Whatever the definition, variability presents a serious obstacle to success. Unfortunately, all too often little thought is given to it ... as was demonstrated by Walter Havisham in the previous chapter.

You may recall that tiresome old Fred Smith provided Walter with a seemingly simple problem (a single processing machine, i.e., one that performed a polishing operation) in which the data presented were restricted to *averages* (*average* arrival rate and *average* processing rate). Walter performed a few simple calculations in his head and voiced his answer – while claiming that the problem itself was simple, particularly for a Harvard grad.

When Fred told Walter that he was missing a critical point, he was referring to the fact that averages are, in many *if not most* cases, misleading. At the very least, they do not provide the information necessary to make an informed decision. As important, if not more so, is the *variability* of the metric (e.g., the *variability* of job arrivals, and the *variability* of processing times).

I cannot help but recall the advice given to a colleague of mine by a financial planner some years ago. The planner noted that the *average* return in the stock market has been, over a period of a hundred years, seven (7) percent a year. The planner even showed my friend an article by Warren Buffett in which Buffett – the fabled "Oracle of Omaha" – stated that you should expect a 6 to 7 percent annual return (on the stock market) *over the long run*.

My colleague, using her computer and a spreadsheet, ran some figures. It seemed a sure bet that her 500,000 dollars in savings would double in just ten years if she placed it in a tracking fund (one that replicates the performance of the stock market). Unfortunately, her confidence was founded on the implied promise of a 7 percent *average* return.

The 500,000 dollars she invested in that fund in 2007 was reduced *by half* by 2009 (during the financial crisis of 2007-2009, the S&P 500 lost approximately 50 percent of its value). She had failed to consider variability, and her financial planner was either ignorant of variability or had chosen to not mention it. Her plans, by the way, of taking early retirement were abruptly changed.

Clearly, we need more than averages if we hope to make an informed decision. In particular, we need to have some knowledge of, and be able to estimate, *variability*.

A particularly useful statistic that may be employed to estimate variability is that of the *Coefficient of Variability*, denoted as *CoV*. To compute the CoV of any metric we must be provided with, or collect a "sufficient" amount of data with regard to the mean and standard deviation of the appropriate data set (e.g., the mean and standard deviation of stock market returns over a "sufficient" time period). That statistic will be presented, and illustrated, later in this chapter. First, however, let's first examine *the impact of complexity on variability*.

Complexity's Impact On Variability

The greater the complexity of the system or process, the greater will be its impact on the variability of the outcomes. In other words, *complexity* **induces** *variability* **and does so throughout the entirety of the system**. As one example, consider the maintenance specifications employed in the preventive (as well as unscheduled) maintenance or repair of a complex machine (e.g., a lithography machine within a semiconductor fab, radar system on a military aircraft, or an MRI machine in a hospital).

The more complex the specification, the longer it will take to complete the maintenance or repair. The more complex the specification, the more likely it is that mistakes will be made, or that pauses will ensue as a consequence of attempts to decipher the meaning of one or more steps. Further, if one maintenance crew (e.g., such as the night crew) is less well-trained (or less proficient, or less dedicated) than another, the difference (the variability) in performance between crews will increase.

The same outcome (an increase in variability) will occur in the development and fielding of a product (e.g., a new laser printer, a new weapon system) or a change in the business processes of a firm or organization. In these instances, however, there may not be (and likely will not be) a way to measure the degree of variability induced by complexity. Or, stated another way, there may be no way to scientifically determine the complexity of the matter under consideration. This is a consequence of two factors:

- Each of the steps of the development/fielding – or change in business processes – occur but once (or a statistically insufficient number of times).

- There may be no meaningful way in which to compare results with that of the development and fielding of a *truly* similar product (e.g., the development and fielding of laser weapon system is dissimilar to that of a more conventional system such as a multiple-launch rocket weapon system from the 60s).

This may be best understood by providing an illustration of the steps involved in the computation of the Coefficient of Variability. (Relax, this is not going to hurt.)

Computation Of The Coefficient Of Variability

The Coefficient of Variability, denoted as CoV, is determined by:
- recording the raw data associated with the specific metric under investigation,
- determining both the mean and standard deviation of that data, and then
- dividing the standard deviation by the mean of the data.

This may be understood by means of a numerical illustration. Assume we are interested in the variability of the interarrival times of jobs processed by a specific processing unit (e.g., a tollbooth, a claims processing center, a machine within a production line, a storage depot within a supply chain, or tools needing maintenance). We begin with the first step above; i.e., we simply *record the clock times of the* interarrivals *of the jobs*.

Assume that, at 8:00 a.m., the first job arrives. The next job arrives at 8:15 a.m.; i.e., 15 minutes later. Thus the *interarrival time* for job 2 is 15 (i.e., 15 minutes *after* the previous job). The illustrative data recorded for this hypothetical example are shown in Figure 4.2.

Job	Arrival Time	Interarrival Time	Job	Arrival Time	Interarrival Time
1	8:00 a.m.	n/a	7	10:02 a.m.	14
2	8:15 a.m.	15	8	10:50 a.m.	48
3	8:50 a.m.	35	9	10:58 a.m.	8
4	8:56 a.m.	6	10	11:33 a.m.	35
5	9:40 a.m.	44	11	11:40 a.m.	7
6	9:48 a.m.	8			

Figure 4.2: Job Interarrival Times

The next step is to compute the mean and standard deviation of the data recorded in Figure 4.2; i.e., the mean and standard deviation of the Job Interarrival Times. These statistics may be computed by hand (using formulas found in most any statistics book) or, more easily, on a spreadsheet.

Once we accomplish those calculations, we will find that the mean of the interarrival times in Figure 4.2 is 22 minutes and its standard deviation is 16.613 minutes. Dividing the standard deviation by the mean (16.612/22) gives a value of 0.755 – *the coefficient of variability*. Thus, CoV = 0.755.

The larger the value of CoV (i.e., the coefficient of variability), the greater the variability of the job interarrivals. In practice [Hopp, W. J. & Spearman, M. J. (2008)] it is sometimes assumed that a CoV value of less than 0.75 indicates *low variability*, while a value between 0.75 and 1.33 is considered *moderate variability*. If the CoV is greater than 1.33, we have *high variability*. Some simulation software packages have, as a default value, a CoV of 1.0. (As a personal note, I have witnessed *numerous* real-world systems – particularly within semiconductor fabs, solar cell manufacturing firms, and aircraft and military weapon systems maintenance – in which the CoVs were 10 or more. I suppose that should be considered *extreme variability* but it is far more common than some textbooks or simulation software might lead you to believe).

To recap, we find the mean and standard deviation of the data and then divide the standard deviation by the mean to determine the coefficient of variability (CoV). *This statistic serves as a proxy for an indication of the complexity of a given system* – much like a person's blood pressure provides an indication of hypertension.

Using the CoV statistic, you can actually observe any increases or decreases in the complexity of a system – given, of course, that it is possible to collect the necessary data. For example, if we believe that the complexity of a given process step is unnecessarily complex, we could (and should) measure its CoV before and after any attempt to remove *Unnecessary* Complexity. If it decreases, we may be on the right track. If, however, it increases, we are likely pointed in the wrong direction.

It should be noted that, in certain instances, various schemes employed to improve performance (e.g., Lean manufacturing, Theory of Constraints) have only served to *increase* variability – and thus diminish *overall* performance. A few examples of this will be discussed and illustrated later in the book. For example, it will be shown how the removal of a constraint which should – according to conventional wisdom – be a "good thing," may actually *negatively* impact the performance of a system – unless the obstacles to success are considered. (This is due, in part, to a lack of appreciation and emphasis on variability.)

Unfortunately, while most firms and organizations characteristically collect massive amounts of data, they routinely fail to realize the critical importance of the collection of *the data necessary to compute variability*. They remain, in too many instances, blissfully ignorant of the impact of *Unnecessary* Complexity on the variability

— *and, in particular, its propagation* — throughout their systems.

And they invariably (no pun intended) pay the price for that lack of awareness.

The coefficients of variability that should be measured and recorded in a system such as a production line or supply chain include but are not limited to:

- Job/task interarrival times
- Scheduled maintenance times
- Unscheduled maintenance times
- Processing station utilization
- Processing station availability
- Transport time (e.g., from one station to another)

If these CoVs decrease when a scheme (e.g., Lean, Six Sigma, Theory of Constraints, etc.) is introduced in an attempt to enhance the operation of a system, we may assume that it is possible the scheme has improved the performance of the system. If, however, the CoVs either increase or remain about the same, the scheme employed may actually be counterproductive. Again, it must be stressed that *some schemes — intended for the enhancement of a systems performance can, if they fail to consider The Three Obstacles, actually make matters worse.*

There are, of course, reasons other than *Unnecessary* Complexity for the variability of a particular system to be excessive. Some of the most common of these are described in the following section.

Causes Of *Excessive* Variability

As has been discussed, *Unnecessary* Complexity — in

terms of such matters as the design, number of motions, components, or the configuration of a given system – *is almost certain to induce Excessive* Variability in a given system and negatively impact its performance, but there are numerous other causes of *Excessive* Variability. The most typical – and detrimental – of these are discussed below.

<<<<>>>>

Indecision: Indecision is one of the most prevalent causes of variability – including *Excessive* Variability. Marvin, the squirrel so heartlessly squashed by Walter Havisham, was a victim of his own indecision. That indecision resulted in him racing back and forth – and getting nowhere. Individuals, firms, and organizations beset by indecision experience similar results. Their indecision accomplishes little, other than *Excessive* Variability.

Unfortunately, even when "the indecisive" make a decision, it's amazing how many times it's wrong.

<<<<>>>>

Chasing fads and fashions: As has been discussed earlier, individuals, firms, and organizations too often seek what they hope might be a cheap, quick-and-easy solution to their problems. There are a host of management gurus that are more than willing to provide their services – services centered on the introduction and implementation of the latest, greatest, sure-fire, quick-and-easy solution. In some instances the fad that is implemented may actually appear to be providing improvement. In the vast majority of instances, however, that improvement is *transient* simply, for example, as a result of the Hawthorne Effect [Roethlisberger, F. J., & Dickson, W. J. (1939)]. The cycle is then repeated, and another fad is introduced.

What is so depressing about the search for a quick-and-easy answer is that so many individuals, firms, and organizations never seem to learn. They must have missed the truly profound life message provided in the comic strip, *Peanuts* (by Charles Schultz). The strip's eight-year old Lucy van Pelt periodically assures the nine-year old Charlie Brown that – *despite all previous instances* – she will, *this time*, hold a football while he place-kicks it. She persuades the gullible Charlie Brown to trust her. When he runs up to kick the ball, she – at the very last second – pulls the ball away and Charlie Brown flies into the air, before falling on his backside.

Lucy does this over and over again and yet Charlie Brown *always* falls for the trick. The analogy between Lucy's promises and that of a management guru's assurances should be obvious. Yet, like Charlie Brown, individuals, firms, and organizations never seem to learn. Naively trusting that the next fad will work, they implement it and, like Charlie Brown, they find themselves on their backsides.

<<<<>>>>

Conflicting Goals and Objectives: I have been witness to a depressing number of firms and organizations in which the primary cause of *Excessive* Variability was "simply" that of the establishment of *too many goals*, and a subsequent focus on their associated (meaningless or counterproductive) metrics. One firm I dealt with, in particular, seemed to be absolutely obsessed with the establishment of *teams* (designated as "factory performance" teams), each tasked with the accomplishment of various (often ill or improperly defined) goals and objectives.

THE THREE OBSTACLES

This obsession with teams, teamwork, team leadership, team wisdom, team building, team innovation, team culture, team size, team member selection, team coaching, team morale, team interrelationships, team passion, *ad nauseam* ... probably shouldn't have been a surprise. The firm's senior vice president of manufacturing, I was later informed, had a collection of more than 50 books on the subject of teams in his bookcase and – according to a persistent rumor – has just recently hired a writer (or perhaps a *team* of writers) to ghost-write "his own" book on teams.

The very existence of his many teams, however, served to *increase* both the *Unnecessary* Complexity and *Excessive* Variability that permeated his firm – from top to bottom. In an earlier book I called this company "Muddle, Inc." [James P. Ignizio, J. P. (2009) – see, in particular, pp. 135-137] and, my goodness, did it ever earn that name.

A list of just some of their factory performance teams, and the measures of effectiveness (i.e., their alleged focus) that were established in the real life "Muddle, Inc." follows:

1. LEAN Forward Team – with an emphasis on the *reduction of waste*

2. CANDO Team – responsible for cleaning up factory workplaces and *reducing clutter*

3. Quality Control Team – with an emphasis on the *reduction of defects*

4. Throughput/Capacity Team – responsible for *maintaining factory throughput* (i.e., achieving a

specified flow of jobs per unit time through the factory)

5. Cycle Time Reduction Team – with the goal of *reducing factory cycle time* (i.e., speeding up the rate of production)
6. Cost Reduction Team – emphasis on *reducing funds expended*
7. Equipment Maintenance Team – *increase the availability (i.e., up-time) of the factory's workstations*
8. Factory Utilization Team – *reduce the idle time of machines and workers* (their goal was to achieve a utilization of 90 percent or more)
9. Spare Parts Team – determine *number and types of spare parts* to maintain in inventory
10. Metrics Team - *collect the data in support of the numerous factory performance measures*

Read the above list carefully, perhaps several times. Realize that, while each of the teams (and their goals/objectives) may seem reasonable (although the Factory Utilization Team's goal is both totally unrealistic *and* counterproductive), *they are each in conflict with one or more of the other teams' goals.*

For example, the Lean Forward Team wants to reduce waste. One of the proxies they chose was the *reduction of (supposedly unnecessary) inspection steps*. This is, however, in direct conflict with the Quality Control Team, which sought to *increase inspection steps* so as to (supposedly) reduce defects.

The Quality Control Team has other conflicts; e.g., with the Cycle-time Reduction Team. Since cycle time may be decreased by reducing process and inspection steps, the goals of these two teams are in conflict.

And then consider the conflict between the Cost Reduction Team and the Spare Parts Team. Increasing spare parts, even if needed, obviously increases cost. And simply making an across-the-board cut in spare parts – as proposed by the Cost Reduction Team – fails to consider the differing need and impact of the various types of spares. Consequently, there were several heated arguments between these two teams, one of which came close to a physical confrontation.

Again, every one of the factory performance teams has one or more conflicts with others.

Each team in Muddle, Inc. is focused on a metric (too often arbitrary, too often simplistic) by which it is measured, and each of these metrics may conflict with what *should be the overall goal* of simply improving *overall factory performance* (in virtually any production line or supply chain, the most appropriate measure of performance is that of the Load Adjusted Cycle Time Efficiency, or LACTE [Ignizio, J. P. (2009). pp 183-189]). Instead, each team worked in isolation, focused on their particular performance metric, and remained ignorant of a rational, overall, effective goal. There was no single point of oversight – as a consequence, as will be discussed, of a serious case of *Intellectual Myopia*.

Before leaving this subtopic, let me add one more fact with regard to the establishment of teams with an excessive, conflicting collection of goals and metrics. In the firm just discussed, Team 7 (the Equipment Maintenance Team) focused almost exclusively on speeding up maintenance events. The approach used by the Equipment Maintenance Team was to hold periodic practice sessions (which, on the surface, would seem to be a good idea).

As a consequence of their practice, the time required to perform a maintenance event – *as outlined in its maintenance specification* – was definitely reduced. They failed, however, to ever address (or even be aware of) the impact of their most crucial maintenance problem: unclear, incomplete, incorrect, and frustratingly ambiguous maintenance specs. As a consequence, the Equipment Maintenance Team, for the most part, simply managed to *reduce the time required to achieve lousy and short-lived results.* (It might also be noted that automation, *if it is the automation of a flawed scheme*, simply achieves lousy results faster.)

<<<<>>>>

Underestimating the Impact of Maintenance on Excessive Variability: Unfortunately, the truly significant impact of maintenance – and particularly maintenance specifications – on system (e.g., factory, supply chains, weapon systems) performance is routinely ignored or severely underestimated. In my more than half-century career, I've served as a consultant to over one hundred firms and, in most of them, the importance – and far reaching impact – of maintenance had not been appreciated. In a disturbing number of these firms/organizations, maintenance was treated as if it was just part of "housekeeping," almost as if the mopping of floors or the emptying of wastebaskets was of the same level of importance as the maintenance of a complex weapon system.

In one firm (good old Muddle, Inc.) I discovered that there wasn't even a maintenance department. While the firm had a long list of departments, there wasn't *any* mention of a maintenance department on that list. When I asked about this omission, I was told that each group (i.e., each department responsible for a given machine type/processing step) was also responsible for the maintenance of that particular type of machine. While there is nothing inherently wrong with such an approach, it can – particularly in a firm like Muddle, Inc. – be problematic if the importance of maintenance is either unappreciated or ignored.

I soon discovered that the topic of maintenance (and, in particular, maintenance specifications) wasn't considered to be all that significant. I received, in fact, the distinct impression that the development, writing, and evaluation of maintenance specifications was considered a "punishment" or – at the very least – an impediment to promotion. (No one that I talked to could remember anyone ever being given an award for his or her maintenance specs at the weekly award ceremonies held by the firm ... which included such awards as holding onto the handrail when walking up or down the stairs).

This lack of appreciation of the impact of maintenance, and of the desperate need for establishment of C4U-compliant maintenance specifications (i.e., **C**lear, **C**omplete, **C**orrect, **C**oncise, and **U**nambiguous specs) is, in a surprising number of instances, the single most crucial factor negatively impacting performance. This is true whether the system of interest is a military weapon system, semiconductor fab, electrical utility grid, supply line, business process, or even a computer code.

In other words, you must realize that unclear, incomplete, incorrect, non-concise, and ambiguous specifications, documentation, or orders are actually another representation of *Unnecessary* Complexity.

Why is maintenance so important? Because improper maintenance (which is so often caused by poorly written maintenance specs) increases the *Excessive* Variability within a given system, and because that variability *is propagated throughout the system* ... even to the point where an otherwise well-designed system may fail simply because of the variability induced by a poorly performed maintenance event.

You can, for example, have a fleet of state-of-the-art military aircraft and ships upon which billions upon billions of dollars were spent in their development, and yet have an ineffective air force and navy. Unless those ships and airplanes are combat ready, you have what amounts to a hollow, impotent force.

Consider, as just one example, the aircraft of the United States Marine Corps. According to an April 17, 2016 news story, "... today the vast majority of Marine Corps aircraft can't fly" [Tomlinson, L. & Griffin, J. (2016)].

Here's an excerpt from that story:

> *To get one Hornet* [F-18 Hornet strike fighter] *flying again, Marines at Beaufort stripped a landing gear door off a mothballed museum jet. The door, found on the flight deck of the World War II-era USS Yorktown, was last manufactured over a decade ago.*

The F-18 Hornet problem is one caused by a lack of spare parts. As will be discussed later, this problem was caused, indirectly, by *Intellectual Myopia*, the third obstacle to success. *Intellectual Myopia* was, in this instance, a failure to foresee the impact of budget cuts – which then caused the lack of spare parts which, in turn, impacted maintenance – and then caused *Excessive* Variability (in the down-time of the fleet).

Chapter Summary

One of the major causes of *Excessive* Variability is complexity. Complexity – particularly *Unnecessary* Complexity – will most absolutely induce variability. Variability, in turn, tends to propagate itself through a system – producing unexpected and deleterious results. Examples of this phenomenon will be presented in Chapter 7.

The examples of the causes of *Excessive* Variability are not, however, limited to its inducement by complexity. Indecision, chasing fads, conflicting goals and objectives, and underestimating the impact of a poor maintenance program are a few other examples of the cause of *Excessive* Variability.

In most instances, these factors are actually a consequence of *Intellectual Myopia*. That subject will be discussed in the next chapter.

5. Intellectual Myopia

Imagination is more important than knowledge. For knowledge is limited, whereas imagination embraces the entire world, stimulating progress, giving birth to evolution.
— Albert Einstein

Rotten bosses don't get better. Any strategy that assumes they can is doomed to failure.
— Scott Adams

The Confederate General, Thomas "Stonewall" Jackson, while he may have been on the wrong side of history, is considered by many historians to have been the most accomplished military tactician of the American Civil War. Jackson's Shenandoah Valley campaign in the spring of 1862 is said to be one of the most brilliant in United States, if not world, military history. Here's what a National Park Service website has to say about Stonewall Jackson:

"Jackson managed in less than three months to march his Army of the Valley hundreds of miles and fight a series of engagements (including five pitched battles) in a masterpiece of military art that ultimately created a grand diversion which tied up thousands of Union troops threatening Richmond. ... Jackson's Valley Campaign was an absolute success. In thirty days, Jackson's men covered 350 miles, defeated three Union commands in five battles, caused 5,000 casualties at a loss of

only 2,000 men, and captured much needed supplies" [*National Park Service, "Overview of the 1862 Stonewall Jackson Valley Campaign"*].

What the website may not sufficiently emphasize, however, was the significant role that *maps* played in Jackson's success [Miller, W. J. (1993)]. In March of 1862, Jackson directed Jedediah (Jed) Hotchkiss to make him a *detailed* map of the Shenandoah Valley (and, while doing so, identify all of the most attractive points of offense and defense in that region). Consequently, while Union commanders were fighting in what was – for them – a virtually uncharted region, Stonewall Jackson knew at all times precisely where he was and where to march his troops in anticipation of the next engagement.

Jackson recognized the crucial importance of maps in support of a (successful) military campaign. Good maps reduce uncertainty – particularly in warfare. In other words, the maps Jackson ordered made served to remove *Unnecessary* Complexity – as well as complexity's impact on *Excessive* Variability. In short, by his decision to order the maps, he mitigated the first and second obstacles to success.

General Stonewall Jackson, as reflected by his strategy and tactics during the war, was clearly not inflicted with *Intellectual Myopia*. Not all decision-makers are, however, so enlightened.

Consider, for example, the words of Henry L. Stimson (U.S. Secretary of State, 1929-1933) with regard to intelligence gathering following World War I: "Gentlemen do not open other gentlemen's mail." It was, however, "the opening of other gentlemen's mail" – in the form of deciphering coded messages – that played a significant role in the Allies victory over

Axis forces in World War II.

Gathering intelligence – by means of making maps, breaking codes, or infiltrating the ranks of the enemy – reduces the unnecessary part of *Unnecessary* Complexity. In turn, the reduction of complexity diminishes its influence on variability.

It should be noted that intelligence agencies also employ *Unnecessary* Complexity and *Excessive* Variability to *their* advantage – by means of *weaponizing* them. This (important) concept – the weaponizing of obstacles one and two – will be explored in detail in Chapter 6.

Attributes Of Decision-Makers

Some decision-makers are imaginative, open to change, willing to listen, able to examine advice objectively, capable of acting decisively, and are proactive rather than reactive. Others are not. Like marble statues, they remain unmoved by any and all arguments for change. Such (non-decision) decision-makers exhibit the telltale symptoms of *Intellectual Myopia*.

A decision-maker suffering from *Intellectual Myopia* is at a serious disadvantage with regard to the achievement of his or her goals. In some instances the affliction may be surmounted, *but only if the decision-maker recognizes his or her affliction and takes the steps necessary to overcome his or her Intellectual Myopia*. For those individuals, however, whose affliction is a reflection of their fundamental *nature* (e.g., unimaginative, stubborn, foolish, profoundly egotistic, disorganized, indecisive, reactive, close-minded, fearful of change), there may be little that can be done.

As a consequence, *Intellectual Myopia* is likely to be the most frustrating and most difficult obstacle to surmount. When faced with *Unnecessary* Complexity or *Excessive* Variability (and if their existence has been identified), there are almost always ways in which to either eliminate or at least mitigate their impact. When, however, the decision-maker suffers from *Intellectual Myopia*, the probability of the achievement of success – particularly over the long-term – is reduced ... significantly.

Before discussing how we *might* overcome this obstacle, it is necessary to gain an appreciation of both the symptoms and causes of *Intellectual Myopia*. Some of the most common *symptoms* of *Intellectual Myopia* include:

- Unimaginative (and one should *never underestimate this symptom*)

- Attraction to fads and fashions, coupled with a naïve belief that a quick-and-easy (or "quick-and-dirty") solution is possible – without having, *of course*, to become personally involved

- A personal library filled with books on fads, fashions, self-help, and trendy management (and an abject ignorance of the checkered history of fads and fashions)

- A marked reluctance to make a decision and/or a habit of putting off making decisions

- An over-reliance on the establishment of committees and teams

- The use of committees and teams to avoid making decisions

- Frequent changes or revisions to his/her goals, objectives, mission statements, and measures of effectiveness (i.e., metrics employed to measure performance)
- A focus on the short-term – even at the expense of the long-term

Whereas, the *causes* of *Intellectual Myopia* may, in many cases, be traced to:

- The decision-maker believes that it is safer to avoid making a decision than to make one that may lead to serious consequences. This is also known as the "Do Nothing" syndrome.
- The decision-maker's position may not be all that secure and thus the fear of making a mistake is intensified. This is an alternate manifestation of the "Do Nothing" syndrome.
- The decision-maker may have been "burned" before. Failed promises of quick-and-easy solutions, made in the past, undermines confidence.
- The decision-maker may be wedded to the short-term (which has the most immediate impact on his/her rewards; e.g., bonuses, promotion, etc.), rather than on what should be done now so as to achieve success over the long-term.
- Or, quite simply, *Intellectual Myopia* may just be a fundamental part of his or her nature. If this is indeed the case, there is no known cure.

I've been asked, numerous times, what to do if you happen to serve as an advisor to an individual afflicted with terminal *Intellectual Myopia*. First of all, I would recommend that you avoid such entanglement ... it's unlikely to end well. If you can't escape that assignment then I would advise you to consider looking for another job. There are few experiences more frustrating – even to the point of affecting one's health – than working for someone with a terminal case of *Intellectual Myopia*.

Fortunately, only a relatively small portion of CEOs and top-level managers in the private sector suffer from *Intellectual Myopia*. This also holds true for senior military officers, at least those whose promotions were on merit rather than politics. Based on my personal experience and decades of observation, I'm sorry to say that one area in which *Intellectual Myopia* verges on being epidemic is among politicians, particularly the career politicians (of any stripe) in Congress.

Imagine That!

One of the most important attributes – *possibly the most important* – of a successful leader is *imagination*. Recall Einstein's quote from the title page of this chapter: "*Imagination is more important than knowledge. For knowledge is limited, whereas imagination embraces the entire world, stimulating progress, giving birth to evolution.*"

An unimaginative decision-maker is a danger to himself or herself, as well as the future of his or her firm, organization, or nation. Some decision-makers haven't, for example, evidently ever seen or read *The Wizard of Oz*. It's no wonder they lack imagination. Recall that the catalyst for the book is *a tornado* ... a tornado that carries Dorothy and her dog, Toto, to the Emerald City.

Dorothy lived in Kansas ... a state that is part of what is known as "Tornado Alley." Nebraska, by the way, is adjacent to Kansas, and also part of Tornado Alley. Roughly 1,000 tornados touch down each year in our country. Most of these are in Tornado Alley – *the most tornado prone region in the entire world.* Citizens of the region encompassed by Tornado Alley, recognizing the danger they are in, routinely construct steel-reinforced safe rooms in their houses, or secure underground tornado shelters.

Then there's the U.S. Air Force. Half and sometimes more of our nation's so-called Doomsday planes are housed at the Offut air base in ... wait for it ... Nebraska, i.e., *in the heart of Tornado Alley.* The Doomsday planes are converted Boeing 747 aircraft with reinforced airframes designed for protection against EMP (Electromagnetic Propagation) and the intense heat generated by a nuclear explosion. They also incorporate a five-mile-long trailing wire antenna that allows communication with our nation's nuclear-capable submarines. These craft serve as aerial command centers in the event of a national emergency. *They are essential.* To accomplish their purpose, however, they must be flight-ready.

On June 16, 2017 a tornado struck the Offut air base in Nebraska. Its two Doomsday planes were damaged and put out of action. Another Doomsday plane was undergoing major maintenance in San Antonio. As consequence, only one of our nation's four Doomsday planes was – at least theoretically – flight ready ... and only that one would be ready until repairs and maintenance were accomplished on the other three.

How could this possibly happen? It was known that a storm was approaching. Both of the Doomsday planes in Nebraska were pulled into hangers in advance of the storm. These hangers, however, weren't designed to accommodate a plane the size of these converted Boeing 747s, and thus *their tails were left hanging out* ... and a target for the tornado of June 16th: Something clearly not anticipated for planes based in Tornado Alley.

Anticipation requires Imagination.

Digitize This!

While it is unlikely that an individual inflicted with *Intellectual Myopia* will rise to the position of CEO, it does happen. Consider, for example, one or more CEOs of Eastman Kodak in the 1990s. Eastman Kodak was, almost from its launch, a highly successful firm. From the company's founding in 1880 through most of the 20th Century, it was the forerunner in film and cameras.

In the early 1980s, a new player in film appeared: Fuji. Fuji not only undercut Kodak in price, its film was considered to be equivalent, in quality. Eastman's Kodak's CEO from 1990 to 1993 was allegedly convinced that the Kodak "brand" was so powerful that it would not be necessary to reduce the price of Kodak film to better compete with Fuji, or to lower prices so as to drive Fuji from the market. That was the first mistake ... Fuji film prospered.

To make matters worse, the CEO didn't appear to appreciate the significance of the digital camera – even though it was Kodak scientists that invented that device. Instead, the CEO evidently assumed that the firm's high profit-margin film business would continue to be the focus of Eastman Kodak.

Without a full commitment to the digital world, Kodak's fortunes continued to fall. In 2012 the firm filed for bankruptcy. Kodak failed, at least in large part, due to *Intellectual Myopia* – particularly by Kodak's senior-level management's apparent lack of imagination and evident belief that a firm's brand would protect it from disruptive ideas, events, and developments.

I'll Think About That Tomorrow

Scarlet O'Hara's famous quote ("I'll think about that tomorrow") from the movie, *Gone With The Wind*, serves to encapsulate one of the most common symptoms of *Intellectual Myopia*: a short-term focus. If awards were given for short-term thinking, one nominee should – in my opinion – be the group of "geniuses" that designed most of the world's nuclear power plants. Whatever your opinion of nuclear power, consider the following summary of a recent article published in the *Wall Street Journal* [Houston-Waesch, M. (2017)]).

There are more than 450 nuclear facilities in the world today. It was well known, when they were constructed, that each had a limited life. More than half the world's nuclear power plants have now reached their end-of-life dates. Only 17 plants have, to date, been decommissioned – but some 160 more now await demolition and that's proving to be a massive job. A major problem now facing the demolition teams is a consequence of the *Intellectual Myopia* that afflicted those who conceived, designed, and constructed those facilities. *Specifically, plants were built with no apparent thought of, or regard to, their dismantling.*

As just one example, many (if not most) builders failed to leave any instructions for decommissioning. Another is the lack of thought given to the design of the facilities. Consider the following quote from the referenced WSJ article "Looming over them (*the engineers in charge of decommissioning*) were 320 tons of radioactive steel covered by a lid that was *way bigger than any of the factory's doorway*s." One has to read the WSJ article to gain a full appreciation of the magnitude of the (unnecessary) problems left by *Intellectual Myopia*.

There's an even bigger potential problem with the world's nuclear power plants; one that hasn't received nearly the attention it deserves. This is the matter of how to deal with local or regional power shutdowns. In the event of a severe electrical grid anomaly or a local blackout, nuclear reactors are designed to automatically shut themselves down. *But they still require electrical power for their cooling systems.* That backup power is provided by diesel-powered generators – *but these are only required to store enough diesel fuel on hand to keep the generators running for one week.*

So, what happens in the event of an EMP (Electromagnetic Pulse Attack)? An EMP attack could (and likely would) cause an electrical grid collapse that lasts far more than a week. After the backup generators run out of fuel, however, the reactor cores will start to melt down. An enormous amount of radiation will be released into the atmosphere and travel with the prevailing weather patterns ... and present a threat far greater than the failed Chernobyl nuclear power plant (a 30-km radius around Chernobyl won't be safe for humans for 20,000 years). Imagine having to wait for 20,000 years to visit the Rock & Roll Hall of Fame in Cleveland!

Sound overdramatic? Don't count on it. Use your imagination.

I Don't Care Syndrome

Sometimes the "I'll think about that tomorrow" syndrome is actually a manifestation of the "I don't care" mentality. There is absolutely no intention, for those of the "I don't care" persuasion, of doing what's right and best for their employees, colleagues, group, firm, or organization. They simply make their decisions and pursue the actions *that benefit them*.

Over a professional career of more than a half-century, there are two individuals that are in a close race for the most self-centered individuals I, personally, have ever encountered. One (Mr. X) was a senior level manager in a major firm. The other (Professor Y) was an academician/administrator at a highly respected American university.

Every decision made, every action taken, and every word spoken by Mr. X appeared to have been carefully planned, solely to advance his career – even at the expense of his firm, his "friends," his family, and his colleagues. Mr. X took credit for every success and blamed someone else – anyone else – for any failure. Even though he was well aware that his decisions would be (and were) detrimental to his firm, he pursued them ... and punished those who did not agree.

Professor Y was adept at making friends with those (and only those) that might advance his career. While Y's teaching and research were, to be extremely generous, marginal, his schmoozing ability was exceptional. So, while his colleagues devoted their time and effort to the teaching and research that would benefit their students and their university, Y received undeserved awards, promotions, and raises.

Now, for those readers who have been around the block, you've likely encountered people like Mr. X and Professor Y. If you have any self-respect and integrity, you'll shake your head in disgust and refuse to follow their lead. Unfortunately, however, the undeserved success achieved by Mr. X and Professor Y can be a temptation to follow in their (tiny, cloven) footsteps. Hopefully, you'll resist that temptation. It isn't worth it.

One Plus One Is Not Necessarily Two

One of the most prevalent symptoms of *Intellectual Myopia* is the *one plus one is two* malady. You can find examples of it everywhere, even – I'm sad to say – in English pubs.

I've spent an awful lot of time in English pubs. But, before you jump to any conclusions, allow me to explain: it's a job requirement. Well, sort of.

In addition to nonfiction, I write mystery novels that take place in England (e.g., *The Last English Village*). Pubs are a great place (you'll have to trust me on this) to discover ideas for story lines. They're also a generous source of free advice – some of it occasionally useful. As one example, while performing research for a mystery titled *The Dog at the Gate*, one of the regulars at the *Perplexed Parson* informed me that, in Britain (or at least his little corner of it), you use the word "jar" rather than "bottle" when referring to the glass container holding that yummy, yeast-extracted staple of British food: Marmite™. I shall forever be in his debt for that piece of advice.

I did, however, receive some questionable advice at the *Sow and Centipede,* a popular pub in the east of England. Rupert, a rabid fan of "vegan friendly" Fuller's London Porter™, asked me how many written words I managed to produce a day. I said that I averaged about 500 words a day. I also confessed that, compared to other writers (e.g., Stephen King's 2,000 words a day), I wasn't achieving anywhere near the 1,000-daily word-count I had hoped for. He next asked me how many hours a day I wrote. I had to admit that, in total, I rarely managed to write for more than four hours a day.

Rupert gave me a pitying look. Shaking his head in bewilderment, he replied: "You say you write 500 words in four hours and you want to produce 1,000 words a day? For pity's sake, mate, if that's what you want then why don't you write eight hours a day?"

Rupert, like most of us, suffers from the naïve belief that *one plus one equals two.* He was quite sure that, if I could produce 500 words in a four-hour time period, I could obviously double that output in double the time. Not only can't I double my output if I attempt to write for eight hours a day, what I produce in those extra four hours has never been to my (or my editor's) satisfaction. I almost always find that I have to spend another three or four hours the next day rewriting those 500 extra words. One "law" that almost always seems to apply is that of "diminishing returns."

Doubling Down

Human beings consistently fall prey to the naïve belief

that *one plus one equals two*; e.g., that by doubling the size of a workforce, you double their output; that doubling your income doubles your happiness, or that doubling your store of military weapons doubles the destruction that can be wrought on your opponent. At one prominent firm, it was decided that departmental leadership was so important that, instead of having one supervisor for each of their departments, they'd have two (and thus the infamous "two-in-a-box" system of management was implemented).

Unfortunately, for them, they discovered that combining an overly cautious supervisor with an impetuous one produced some unfortunate, if not disastrous results. Or that two nitwits aren't better, or even equivalent, to one competent individual. Or that the productivity of a "two-in-the-box" team that become romantically involved can suffer ... mightily. (Curiously, the same firm never considered the idea of a "two-in-the-box" CEO.)

At another company it was believed that, by doubling the number of machines in each processing station of their production line, they would (*obviously*, or so they believed) double the factory's output. The result of that enormously costly effort was, instead, a *slower* production line – coupled with *increased defects*. Had they analyzed their situation properly (employing the *nonlinear* functions that actually serve to estimate production line output), they would have been aware that their scheme would lead – for their factory – to dreadful results. Instead, the last I heard, they've embarked on what they call a "Hurry-Up Campaign." Yeah, that should go well.

The *one plus one is two* delusion has also become

apparent (although, evidently, not fully appreciated or understood) in the conception, design, and development of new weapon systems. Consider, for example, a military aircraft − costing $130M, if not more, per copy. If, as has been reported, only one of six of those aircraft were able to get themselves airborne during an exercise "designed to test their readiness," then rather than having a force of *six* strong, you actually have a massively expensive force of just *one* [Dillow, C. (2016)].

Academia is another place where one plus one is not necessarily two. One course in electrical engineering plus one course in, say, the music of the Beatles (and that's an actual course, by the way, at several universities − you can even, at one illustrious British university, get a Masters degree in The Beatles) is not equal to two serious courses. If you hope to obtain a well-paying job upon graduation, it's unlikely that the Beatles course will add much, if anything, to your engineering degree (unless, I suppose, your job interview is conducted by a truly dedicated Beatles fan ... a dying breed).

Then there's the matter of medicine. If one type of pill (say warfarin) reduces your likelihood of blood clots and another (a sulfa drug) relieves your infection, that combination of two "good" things produces a possibly lethal interaction (by increasing the effect of the warfarin).

As one last example of *one plus one does not necessarily equal two*, consider today's automobiles. The insurance industry has assured us that *safer cars equals lower insurance rates*. *Automobile manufacturers* tell us that, with the introduction of such new safety systems as autonomous braking, backup cameras, navigation systems, lane-departure warnings, and HUDs (heads-up-displays), *new cars are definitely safer*. Yet, because of these new safety systems, many (if not most) insurance firms *are raising prices*.

Why? According to a *Wall Street Journal* article of April 3, 2017 [Niedzwiecki, S. (2017)], "new cars with crash prevention technology and Advanced Driver Assistance Systems (ADAS) are causing auto insurance rates to rise dramatically." The added safety features are often located on the parts of the car most prone to accidents (e.g., the bumper) and when the safety features need replacing, the costs can be five times that of cars without such features. Consequently, two good things add up to one really bad outcome for the car owner.

The problem, and it is a serious one, with the *one plus one is two* belief is that it is a trap that is so easy to fall into – unless you take pains to avoid it. *The linear mindset, inherent in human thought, simply does not deal well with the real world and its inherent nonlinearity*. Decision-makers, whether they are individuals, corporations, or organizations must always take this into account if they are to avoid the pitfalls of the *one plus one is two* syndrome.

I'll close this section with a quote from a *Harvard Business Review* article [de Langhe, B., Puntoni, S. & Larrick, R. (2017)]:

> *Decades of research in cognitive psychology show that the human mind struggles to understand nonlinear relationships. Our brain wants to make simple straight lines. ... But in business there are many highly nonlinear relationships, and we need to recognize when they're in play. This is true*

> *for generalists and specialists alike, because even experts who are aware of nonlinearity in their fields can fail to take it into account and default instead on relying on their gut. But when people do that they often end up making poor decisions.*

For our purposes we can consider the human tendency to think linearly in a nonlinear world as yet another example of one of the obstacles to success: a type of *Unnecessary* Complexity. But then *Unnecessary* Complexity, as will be discussed in the next chapter, does have its uses.

6. Weaponization Of The Three Obstacles

*The whole secret lies in confusing our enemy,
so that he cannot fathom our true intent.*
— Sun Tzu, *The Art of War*

*No enterprise is more likely to succeed than one
concealed from the enemy until it is ripe for execution.*
- Niccolò Machiavelli, *The Prince*

Patrick (not his real name) had somehow (and that's another story) managed to avoid flunking out of university and was in the first semester of his junior year. Patrick was enrolled in a course on basic probability and statistics and his poor grades on his tests and homework in that course had him teetering on the verge of failing – and subsequently flunking out of school. His only hope of passing rested on a research paper submitted at the end of the semester.

After finishing grading about half the papers that had been handed in, the course instructor picked up Patrick's submission. On its cover were the paper's title, Patrick's name, his email address, and the date of submission. Turning to the next page, the instructor noticed two rather peculiar things. The type was of a conspicuously different font than on the title page and the header on every page that followed had a name other than Patrick's. What Patrick had handed in was a research paper – submitted two years earlier by another student – and now with nothing other than a different cover page.

According to the university's honor code, Patrick should have been expelled from the university. He wasn't. The next year Patrick retook the same course – but this time with a different professor. Once again his passing grade depended upon the grade he would receive on the course's final paper. Once again he turned in the same fraudulent paper he had submitted to the course's previous instructor, the previous year. Once again, he was caught cheating.

So, what does this vignette have to do with the subject of this chapter; i.e., the weaponization of the first two obstacles? *The answer is that Patrick's cheating is an excellent example of how **not** to weaponize the three obstacles.*

Specifically, Patrick failed to add any degree of complexity or variability to his tactics. His cheating was immediately obvious (e.g., the header with another student's name remained on the paper) and his "tactic" lacked any degree of variability (e.g., he did exactly the same thing in exactly the same course).

Sadly, the university's response also didn't vary; Patrick was given nothing more than a warning and allowed to substitute another (and much easier) course for the one in which he had so blatantly cheated twice. Enough, however, of Patrick's example of how **not** to weaponize the first two obstacles to success. Let's examine how it is, and should be, done.

The Fumblerooski

Recall that the *apparent Unnecessary* Complexity of

Soviet era shopping, as well as the massive complexity of our nation's IRS rules, was discussed in Chapter 3. It was noted there that both *Unnecessary* Complexity and *Excessive* Variability might be used *to one's advantage*. In a competitive situation – such as sports, warfare, business, politics, or finance – we can oftentimes weaponize the first two obstacles and inflict them on our opponent.

Our objective, in doing so, is to deceive the opponent, confuse him, and thus encourage (i.e., trick) him into making the wrong decision. This may be illustrated by means of a simple example from the game of (American) football.

There are two teams on the field: the offense (the team with the football at any given moment) and the defense (the team seeking to stop the offense from scoring). Neither team wants the other to know what they plan to do on any play. This deception is often accomplished – by both sides – by means of the *introduction of what appears* **to the opponent** as *Unnecessary* Complexity and *Excessive* Variability.

One example is a scheme that may be employed by the offense, the so-called "fumblerooski" play. The offense, for example, may want the defense to believe that this is a running play to the right when, in actuality, it is a running play to the left – employing an offensive player that normally does not even touch the ball. Here's how the play unfolds:

- The center snaps the ball to the quarterback.
  - The quarterback pretends to fumble the ball when, in actuality, he intentionally places the ball on the ground.

- Then the quarterback and his running backs run to their right (drawing the defensive players, who believe either the quarterback or one of the running backs has the ball, to their left).
- In the meantime, one of the offense's guards (who, normally, does not touch the football) scoops up the ball and runs to his left.
- If the defense has been sufficiently deceived (i.e., they have been misdirected), the offensive guard (now carrying the ball) should be able to advance the ball.

The fumblerooski will succeed only if the offense has *deceived* the defense. The weaponization of *Unnecessary* Complexity and *Excessive* Variability is thus a form of deception. Deception, in turn, has been employed for millennia in warfare. To quote from *The Art of War*, "The whole secret [i.e., to success in battle] lies in confusing the enemy, so that he cannot fathom our true intent."

As such, the weaponization of the first two obstacles to success is – on the surface – straightforward: *Present the opponent with what he perceives as complex* and, to further confuse him, *include variability*. A few examples of how this type of weaponization has been employed follow.

WW2: North Africa Campaign

In the North Africa Campaign, British forces significantly outnumbered the Axis forces: forces led by Field Marshall Erwin Rommel (whose leadership during this campaign led to his nickname of "The Desert Fox"). To counter that disadvantage, Rommel employed a deception that consisted of (*in the eyes of his opponent*) both *Unnecessary* Complexity and *Excessive* Variability so as to fool the British into believing that his force was much larger than it actually was. The British, repeatedly falling for this deception, would split their forces and, in doing so, allow Rommel to win battle after battle.

In one tactic used to deceive the British, Rommel would order his *trucks* to proceed to a given area in which they would drive round and round, creating great clouds of dust that could be, *and were meant to be*, seen by the British. British commanders assumed the dust was being created by the movement and entrenchment of Rommel's *tanks* ... and prepared to attack that area. Having deceived the British, Rommel would move his tank columns into flanking positions and wait for the Brits to fall into his trap.

The Business World

While it seems reasonable to anticipate deception in warfare (any military leader that doesn't won't – or shouldn't – last long), the use of deception in the business world may seem unrealistic. Trust me, it isn't. And not all of it is illegal ... or even unethical.

In many instances a small business wants to appear to be large (e.g., similar, in many respects, to Rommel's desire to have the British think that his forces were larger than they were). Generally, the bigger you are (or appear to be), the more respected – or, at least, the more feared – you are.

In the days when businesses were housed strictly in brick-and-mortar buildings, it wasn't easy to pretend to be large. In today's world, where so many businesses are represented as Internet addresses, it is far easier to appear larger than you actually are – particularly if you're not concerned with just how you might achieve that.

This can be accomplished by means of well-designed websites and blogs – coupled with the use of SEOs (Search Engine Optimization). Ads can be purchased at relatively reasonable rates (e.g., on Facebook and Google) to further the impression of size. And, if you wish to pursue a less than honest means, *positive reviews can be purchased* (often at a rate of just $5 a review) – such as was the case with product reviews on Amazon [Weise, E. (2015)]. Then there's Todd Rutherford who claims to have made, in just one month, $28,000 by writing fake reviews: $99 for one, $499 for 20, and $999 for 50 [Carlson, N. (2012)].

When the number of such reviews is large, and when they vary – so as to disguise their true nature – somewhat in wording, they have been weaponized. This can be (and has been, and continues to be) augmented by the purchase of negative reviews directed at a competitor's product page.

Weaponization Of Revenue Generation

An increasingly popular way for local governments to generate revenue is by means of unnecessarily complex traffic laws coupled with excessive variability in their enforcement, interpretation, and areas of coverage. In the county that I live in (unofficial motto: *Arrive on vacation; leave on probation*) there are a massive number of ways in which you can receive a ticket for a traffic violation (and no, I haven't *as yet* received one).

Most of these are reasonable (speeding, not

stopping at a stop sign, etc.) but many are for picayune, virtually unknown, offenses. (Evidently, in Massachusetts, gorillas are not permitted in the back seat of your car. I'm still checking to see if they are allowed to sit in the front seat.)

In some small towns in Louisiana, according to the Sunlight Foundation [Shaw, E. (2016)] some localities collect more in traffic fines than in taxes. So, if you are a local government official, the weaponization of traffic laws appears to provide a sure-fire way to "succeed." Such traffic enforcement policies, coupled with the imposition of ticketing quotas on police officers is, indeed, an example of weaponization ... directed against you.

Legal Documents

If you are a lawyer, *Unnecessary* Complexity and *Excessive* Variability are your friends. If not, realize that these two obstacles have definitely been weaponized against you. As an example, consider the following disclaimer used by one firm (Jux Law) at the end of their emails (https://jux.law/sample-email-disclosures-templates-for-email-footers/):

> TO ENSURE COMPLIANCE WITH INTERNAL REVENUE SERVICE CIRCULAR 230, WE INFORM YOU THAT ANY U.S. FEDERAL TAX ADVICE CONTAINED IN THIS COMMUNICATION, INCLUDING ALL ATTACHMENTS, IS NOT INTENDED OR WRITTEN TO BE USED, AND CANNOT BE USED, FOR THE PURPOSE OF (1) AVOIDING PENALTIES UNDER THE INTERNAL REVENUE CODE OR (2) PROMOTING, MARKETING OR RECOMMENDING TO ANOTHER

> PARTY ANY TAX-RELATED MATTER(S) ADDRESSED HEREIN. *Confidentiality Note: This transmission may contain information which is privileged, confidential, and protected by the attorney-client or attorney work product privileges. If you are not the addressee, note that any disclosure, copying, distribution, or use of the contents of this message is prohibited. If you have received this transmission in error, please destroy it and notify me immediately at TwinCitiesFirm.com.*

When a living, breathing, human being whose native language is English reads such a disclaimer, a typical reaction is likely to be: Huh?

"Legalese," the complex, confusing terms and wordings used by lawyers, has a number of purposes ... including its use as a weapon ... and sales tool. The more complex and confusing it is, the more likely the average person will feel pressured into relying on the use of a lawyer in the writing or interpretation of even the simplest legal document. (At one time in human history you could jot down your own will, such as a man in Germany did years ago: "All to wife.")

The weaponization of *Unnecessary* Complexity, coupled with legalese, has enriched many a lawyer ... and politician.

Scientific Papers

Here's the title of a paper that just begs to be read: *A Comparative Study and Evaluation of the Employment of N-tuples in Ontogenic Neural Networks for M-tuple Self-Learning in Transient Hyperspace via Bayesian Classification and Non-Concurrent Self-Alignment.*

Okay, I made that title up. It is, however, representative of the unnecessarily complex titles employed in actual scientific papers (and note that the titles of papers written by teams of medical doctors are often even more obtuse.) Why such *Unnecessary* Complexity?

The answer is simple. In virtually every instance a far simpler, far shorter title could (and should) have been used. Instead, the author (or authors) has employed *Unnecessary* Complexity in an attempt to impress. (In many cases a very slight revision to the paper, coupled with an even more complex title, will also be submitted for publication; i.e., publish or perish.)

As an editor of books, professional journals, and as a reviewer for the articles submitted to such journals, I can assure you that the weaponization of *Unnecessary* Complexity and *Excessive* Variability in the titles of scientific papers is *not* a rare occurrence. And, as a conscientious voter, I can also assure you that the wording on ballots, as discussed in the next section, is also weaponized.

Politics

Deception is rampant in the world of politics, whether local, regional, state, or national. Consider, for example, the wording of survey questions and ballot statements. It is relatively easy to phrase a question or statement so as to virtually guarantee the result you want. Here's a few examples:

- Consider the actual wording of a question with regard to the retirement age of the State of Pennsylvania's judges: *Shall the Pennsylvania Constitution be amended to require that justices of the Supreme Court, judges, and magisterial district judges be retired on the last day of the calendar year in which they attain the age of 75 years?*

The question was worded so that it appeared that the voter is demanding a retirement at age 75 when, in fact, the existing retirement age was age 70. A poll conducted by Franklin and Marshall University found that the question passed as is, but failed when phrased as an *increase* in retirement age [Loeb, P. (2106)].

- In the 2012 vote in Florida, one amendment (proposing property tax breaks) was 640 words long. (Observers also state that the amendments are not "clearly written.")

The misleading, confusing, overly wordy amendments on local, state, or national ballots are almost always – surprise, surprise – designed to slant the results to the desires of those in power.

<<<<>>>>

Another example of the politically motivated weaponization of obstacles one and two include the planting of false stories about one's opponent ... and do so as close to Election Day as possible. This form of *Unnecessary* Complexity can be particularly effective when combined with a campaign of rumors. The rumors can be as wild as possible, and – as is becoming more and more common – don't have to be sourced.

So, if you want to reduce the number of votes cast for Candidate X, you might float such false rumors as:

- "Candidate X was seen beating his daughter's puppy," says an anonymous source.

- "Candidate X bullied a fellow student when they were in kindergarten," say two anonymous sources.

Put out enough of these false allegations and Candidate X's time and resources will be diverted to their denial. Put them out close to Election Day and Candidate X won't even have time to refute them.

Surveys and polls are also a way in which to deceive potential voters. Consider, for example, a poll taken by the Center for Public Relations at the University of Southern California's Annenberg School. The school polled some 900 individuals and was so excited by the results that they immediately filed a press release. In that press release they stated – conclusively – that "Over 80 percent of PR [Public Relations] professionals polled believe WH spokespeople [*Republican appointees*] 'constantly change their views' and 'distort' the truth."

The political leanings of the 900 poll participants were 55.3 percent liberal, 29.6 percent moderate, and just 15.1 percent conservative [West, M. B. (2017)]. Whatever your opinion of President Trump and his spokespeople, it would seem that a poll in which just 15.1 percent of respondents were conservative just might exhibit a slight hint of weaponization. Had, for example, 55.3 percent of the participants been conservative, and just 15.1 percent liberal, I'm fairly confident that the result of the poll would have been quite the opposite.

Chapter Summary

In essence, the weaponization of *Unnecessary* Complexity and *Excessive* Variability involves:

- develop *what appears* to the competitor/opponent to be a complex (or overly complex) set of tactics and, where possible, include what appears to be excessive variability
- develop a set of detailed procedures to carry out the deceptive tactics
- exercise the apparently unnecessarily complex and excessively variable tactics

And always be aware that *Unnecessary* Complexity and *Excessive* Variability can and will be used *against you*.

7. Facts Are Stubborn Things ...

Facts are stubborn things; and whatever may be our wishes, our inclinations, or the dictates of our passions, they cannot alter the states of facts and evidence.
— John Adams, Second President of the United States

The difficulty lies not so much in developing new ideas as in escaping from old ones.
— John Maynard Keynes

On the first day of class of each semester I have, for decades, presented my students with a "pop quiz." It doesn't figure into their final grade; instead, it provides me with a means to better evaluate their "situational awareness," i.e., their familiarity with the world around them and the events that have shaped that world. The first three of the thirty-two questions on that quiz are listed below:

- When and why did WW2 happen?

- During what century was our nation's Revolutionary War fought and who did we gain our independence from?

- When did our nation's astronauts land on the moon?

Each semester the answers I receive are more and more troubling. Listed below are actual responses (and, unfortunately, all too typical in their absurdness) to each of the above questions. (These students are either university seniors or graduate students.)

- "WW2 was fought in the 17th century to protect our country from an invasion by the French."
- "The Revolutionary War was fought *way back* in the 1900s and we gained our independence from Russia." [Italics added.]
- "Sorry, professor, this is a trick question. Our astronauts never landed on the moon. The pictures shown on television were made on the back lots of Hollywood studios."

As mentioned in Chapter 3, I have some familiarity with the Apollo manned-moon landing program, and I was deployed for several years at Cape Kennedy (the moon landing program's launch site). The fact that some of my students – as well as other Americans – do not believe we landed astronauts on the moon is, to say the least, unsettling. But I suppose it could be worse ... for, example, in Britain.

A 2016 survey of 1,003 Brits found that 52 percent believe the moon-landing story was a hoax [McCrum, K. (2016)]. On the other hand:

- 30 percent believe in ghosts
- 12 percent believe in extraterrestrials
- 10 percent believe in the Loch Ness monster
- 8 percent believe in Fairies
- And then there's the 90 percent of the British population that think rolling a nine-pound round of cheese down a hill (i.e., at the annual

Cooper's Hill cheese rolling contest) is a sport. [I should probably admit that I took the cheese rolling contest survey in a pub in Gloucester.]

In a 1999 survey by Gallup *of Americans* it was found that six percent of the respondents believe the moon-landing program was a deception [Griggs, B. (2009)]. While "just" six percent are convinced the moon landing was a hoax, that's still roughly *18 million* of your fellow citizens. Personally, I'm convinced a wildly disproportionate number of those 18 million serve in congress, or as television news anchors, management gurus, or in DMV offices.

But I digress. The purpose of my outburst was to ask a question pertinent to the subject of this book. Specifically, why are some people so unwilling to change their beliefs even in the face of overwhelming evidence? Why does, for example, a former colleague – a man who, to this day, remains convinced we did not land on the moon – believe that he can solve his firm's supply chain's problems by demanding that his employees "hurry things up." Or that the answer to a problem that has existed for more than a decade in his firm will be cured by forcing his employees to attend a two-hour seminar presented by a motivational speaker who espouses *visualization*.

To solve the myriad of problems in the firm's supply chain (virtually all of which were a result of *Unnecessary* Complexity and *Intellectual Myopia*), the seminar speaker assured his captive audience that all they had to do was to visualize the supply chain as a system of pipes (as in the plumbing system of a house) and *then imagine* that all the "clogs" were cleared. The attendees, for the most part, kept their mouths shut. It was a glassy-eyed bunch that ultimately – after a sprinkling of polite applause – left the auditorium.

For those who find it difficult to let go of their faith in certain management fads, or the advice of motivational speakers, allow me to present a trigger warning for the material to follow:

> *Certain facts, as identified in this chapter, may be cause for consternation among some advocates of various management and manufacturing schemes. Facts can indeed be "stubborn things" from which an escape to a safe place may prove difficult. This discussion will be continued and elaborated upon in Chapter 8 where a detailed examination of the primary reason for the high failure and disappointment rate of such schemes will be posited.*

<<<<>>>>

If anyone wishes to skip the details that follow, I've summarized the findings and listed them in the summary section of this chapter. All others may continue reading ... particularly those who want answers to the two "simple" problems posed by Fred Smith.

<<<<>>>>

Just as a picture may be worth a thousand words, an example that illustrates and clarifies a complex topic may be worth a thousand mathematical symbols and formulas. In this chapter a number of examples that serve to reinforce the material presented in previous chapters are presented. For the most part, graphs and an accompanying discussion will be used in support of these illustrations. For those who desire more details, as well as access to the equations and calculations that support and validate the results, these may be found in the references [Ignizio, J. P. (2009), particularly Chapters 5 and 6.].

Miles Per Gallon?

Let's start off with the mpg consumption rate problem that was presented at the end of Chapter 3. The problem statement was:

> *Assume that you drive a car uphill for 100 miles at a miles-per-gallon consumption rate of precisely one (i.e., one mile per gallon). Then you drive it downhill for another 100 miles, at a rate of 100 mpg. What, Fred asks, is your average mpg rate for that 200-mile trip, i.e., is it approximately (i.e., rounded off to the nearest integer):*
>
> *a. 25 mpg*
>
> *b. 50 mpg*
>
> *c. 2 mpg*
>
> *d. or none of the above?*

While this is, or should be, a remarkably simple problem it has been observed that the majority of individuals answer – all too quickly – with the choice of *b*, i.e., 50 mpg. The correct answer, however, is *c*, i.e., 2 mpg. That result is found when we take the time to formulate the problem.

First, consider the definition of miles per gallon. It is simply the number of miles traveled divided by the gallons of gasoline consumed. Since we traveled uphill 100 miles and then downhill another hundred, the total number of miles driven is 200.

In doing so, we consumed 100 gallons driving uphill and one gallon driving downhill, for a total of 101 gallons. Dividing 200 miles traveled by 101 gallons consumed, the result is 1.98 mpg or, rounded to the nearest integer, 2 miles per gallon.

The key to solving most any problem is to concentrate ... on the big picture. Take a moment before you attempt to find a solution ... like Walter Havisham should have done before venturing his (wrong) answers to the questions posed by Fred Smith.

Fred Smith's Simple Little Problem

Fred Smith's question, presented in Chapter 3, as to the cycle time (average time to complete a job) in a "simple little one stage processing system" was:

> *Jobs arrive at a processing station – one that simply polishes the product and sends it to a delivery station. Jobs (items to be polished) arrive,* **on average***, every five minutes. It takes,* **on average***, two minutes to perform the polishing operation. How long,* **on average***, will it take to complete 100 jobs?*

Before jumping to any conclusions, as Fred's boss did, first read the problem statement carefully. Note that Fred employed the word, *average,* a total of three times. "Average," unfortunately, is one of the most misunderstood and misused words in the English language. Consider, for example, the unfortunate case of Webster Meriwether Martin.

> *It was a brilliant spring day. The sun was shining, the skies a dazzling blue, and birds were chirping. Webster Meriwether Martin could no longer resist temptation. Today, he*

decided, would be a perfect day to hike through the countryside. About 30 minutes into his stroll he arrived at a lovely stream. Webster was desperate to continue his walk, despite the watery obstacle in front of him. Having never learned to swim, he checked his guidebook for information on the stream. It stated that the average depth of the stream was three feet. At a height of six foot-four, Webster concluded that wading this particular stream wouldn't present much of a problem.

Webster removed his brand-new walking boots, tightened the belt on his equally new hiking shorts, and waded into the water. Unfortunately, while the average depth may have been three feet, the depths throughout the stream ranged from about a foot to a scattering of sudden drop-offs of more than ten feet. The (late) Webster Martin was introduced to "the flaw of averages" [Savage, S. L. (2009)] *roughly halfway across the stream.*

But back to Fred's silly little problem: A way to estimate the time to complete 100 jobs is to determine the cycle time of an average job and multiply that by 100. To repeat, we need to determine *cycle time* (not throughput, not cost, not capacity, not defects, etc.).

In order to even venture an educated guess as to the answer to Fred Smith's processing station problem, you must realize that it requires far more than data as to average arrival and processing rates. In fact, the data Fred provided (i.e., average arrival and processing rates) represent only a small portion of the data that determine cycle time ... *and, in fact, are not the most influential* – as explained in the next section.

Cycle Time Determination

The variables that determine cycle time (*for the simple processing system that Fred specified,* i.e., single processing unit, one processor, no batching, and a non-reentrant flow) are:

- *variability* of arrivals at the processing unit (i.e., specifically the *square of the coefficient of variability of interarrivals* at the process step)
- *variability* of the process times of the processing unit (i.e., the *square of the coefficient of variability of effective process times*)
- *average process rate* of the processing unit (i.e., 2 minutes per job – or 0.5 jobs per minute)
- *average arrival rate* of the jobs arriving at the process step (i.e., every 5 minutes – or 0.2 jobs per minute)
- *average availability* of the processing unit
- *average utilization* of the processing unit

Given the values of these variables, and after inserting those values into the appropriate form of what is known as the Pollaczek-Khintchine (or, P-K) equation (equation form, details, and examples are provided in [Ignizio, J.P., (2009)]), we may estimate the cycle time of Fred Smith's "silly little problem." Unfortunately, as mentioned, insufficient information has been provided and thus – as Fred Smith noted – we cannot determine the cycle time of the processing unit (and thus the expected time to process 100 jobs).

We can, however, *assume a range of values for the coefficients of variability* and I will, for sake of discussion, assume that the processing unit is always available (e.g., 100 percent availability). I'll also assume – simply for the purpose of illustration – that the coefficients of variability of both the arrival rates and processing rates, whether increasing or decreasing, remain equal. Under these assumptions, the P-K equation delivers the cycle time results (in minutes) shown in Figure 7-1:

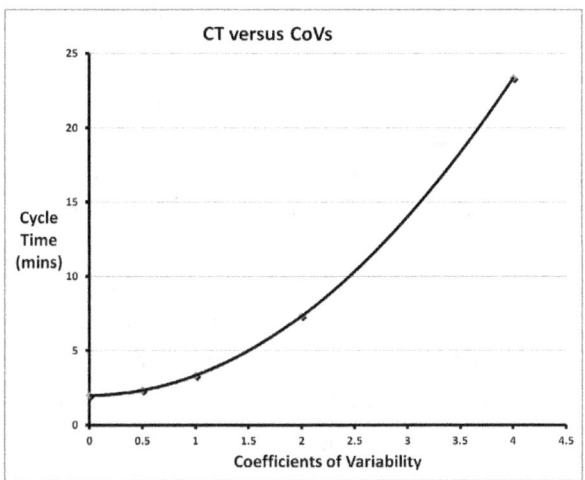

Figure 7.1: Cycle Time versus CoV

When there is *zero variability* (an impossibility in the real world) about the arrival rates or process times, the average time to finish a job is, *theoretically*, 2 minutes (i.e., as Walter Havisham so naively assumed in his response). When there *is* variability (*as there **always** will be*), the average time to finish a job increases, as shown in the graph, *exponentially*. For example, if the CoVs of arrival rates and process times are both 1.0, the average time to finish a job is about 3.33 minutes. When the two CoVs reach values of 4.0, the cycle time climbs to approximately 23.33 minutes.

And what about the use of batches? If we use a simple batching scheme (e.g., such as transfer batching) *the coefficient of variability of arrival rates increases with the size of the batch* and, consequently, this can actually *increase* cycle time [Ignizio, J. P. (2009)].

Even though we may not know the actual values of the coefficients of variability about arrival rates and process times, it should be clear that the cause of Walter Havisham's problem (i.e., the length of time required to process claims) is likely either the variability induced by the use of batches (batches of claims delivered, every four hours, to Unit X) or the variability that exists within Unit X ... or, even more likely, a combination of both. Rather than increasing the workforce in Unit X, a more cost-effective, sustainable method to reduce processing time is to:

- Eliminate batching, or at least reduce the batch size of the claim forms delivered to Unit X (e.g., instead of delivering the claim forms to Unit X every four hours, deliver them every one or two hours).

- Instead of allowing unstructured claimant responses (and thus introducing *Unnecessary* Complexity), establish a standardized claimant response form (e.g., responses to a well ordered, carefully worded and selected list of questions which, in turn, should reduce the inducement of *Excessive* Variability).

An important message to take away from this discussion is that if you want to speed up a production line, supply chain, or business processing system (while also reducing queue sizes), then:

> *Any action that reduces variability will almost always have a greater impact on the reduction of cycle time than any actions that involve such matters as increasing machines (i.e., increasing capacity), or adding workers (i.e., just another way to add capacity). Furthermore, reducing variability is almost always easier, faster, more sustainable, and much less costly than any other approach.*

To put it another way, it is essential to first recognize the existence of the first two obstacles to success in Fred's claim processing system (e.g., *Excessive* Variability as induced by the *Unnecessary* Complexity in the interpretation of the unstructured claimant statement, and the use of batching) and then take the steps necessary to either eliminate or mitigate those obstacles.

Let's return, however, to the idea of *increasing capacity* (i.e., throughput flow) rather than *reducing variability*. After all, isn't that the focus of a number of popular management schemes? I'll examine that matter in the following section.

Increase Capacity (i.e., Throughput Flow) Or Reduce Variability?

Let's recap Fred Smith's simple little problem. It consists of a single processing unit (i.e., a single stage consisting of a single processor). Jobs arrive at the unit every five minutes on average (i.e., an average arrival rate of 0.2 jobs per minute). Processing requires, on average, two minutes (i.e., an average process rate of 0.5 jobs per minute). For sake of discussion, I've assumed that the processing unit's availability is 100 percent (i.e., 100 percent of the time it is up and running) and that the loading on the processor remains the same (i.e., no need to load adjust cycle times).

If we use the P-K equation to determine the cycle time for the processing unit, the result – when the CoVs of both interarrivals and process times are 4.0 – is a cycle time of 23.33 minutes, as previously depicted in Figure 7.1.

If we want to reduce cycle time, we may choose to either increase the processing unit's capacity (i.e., increase throughput, maximum rate of flow) or reduce variability (i.e., reduce the coefficients of variability, now at 4.0 each). To increase capacity (and thus increase throughput), we might consider adding another processor (e.g., machine). The results of such an action would, at least theoretically, be a doubling of capacity (in this particular problem) and would result in a cycle time of five minutes.

Increasing the capacity of a production line, or supply chain, or business process is, in most instances, costly and time consuming. While doubling the number of process units (i.e., a 100 percent increase) in this example reduces cycle time to five minutes, we can see from Figure 7.1 that *by simply reducing the coefficients of variability by just 62.5 percent (from 4 to about 1.5) we can achieve the same cycle time (i.e., 5 minutes) as achieved by a 100 percent increase in capacity*. Such a result is most definitely *not* an anomaly. In short, reducing variability usually provides greater leverage than increasing capacity, and at far less cost.

Reducing variability *to reduce cycle time* is almost

always much faster and much cheaper – and more sustainable – than increasing capacity *to reduce cycle time*. Consider, as an example, a semiconductor fab. A single lithography machine (aka, "tool") can cost tens of millions of dollars [Clarke, P. (2015)] and, in the typical semiconductor fab, there will be multiple lithography tools in any given lithography processing station. Consequently, the addition of just one of these tools – *in an attempt to reduce cycle time via increasing capacity* – will cost far, far more than the cost of an effort (i.e., a well-planned effort) dedicated to reducing variability throughout the production line.

> *If your goal is to reduce cycle time, the reduction of variability will almost always trump increasing capacity – and can be achieved faster, cheaper, and is more sustainable.*

Wrong Assumptions In; Rubbish Out

In Chapter 3, I discussed the matter of my visit to a semiconductor fab ... a newly constructed fab whose performance was far, far worse than their costly, extremely detailed, time-consuming simulation effort had predicted. To refresh your memory, a brief excerpt of that vignette follows:

> *After finishing his impromptu presentation, the manager got to the point – the specific reason why he had asked me to meet with him. While he had a massive, complex, expensive, state-of-the-art facility, its performance was far less than anticipated – or predicted by a costly, time consuming series of computer simulations. In fact, the facility's actual performance was quite dismal despite*

> *all the motivational speakers they had invited and all the sure-fire, quick-and-easy, performance improvement methods they had tried – and it certainly deviated significantly from the spectacular results that had been projected by means of simulation.*

Why, you might ask (and you really should, particularly at this point in the book), didn't the firm's "costly, time consuming, series of simulations" do a much better job of predicting the new semiconductor fab's performance? By now you've probably guessed that at least a few of *The Three Obstacles* must have played a role, and of course you'd be right. After all, that is the title of this book.

The costly, time-consuming simulation package employed by the firm – and, in fact, a software package used by numerous companies and organizations – produced, for the firm in question, problematic results because:

- It relied on a highly detailed (actually an *overly detailed* and thus *unnecessarily complex*) simulation model. (It took days to complete just one simulation experiment.)

- The simulation model employed, as its default setting for the variabilities of each process or inspection step, coefficient of variability values of 1.0 (as did the spreadsheet evaluations used by the firm's analysts).

The default value of 1.0 for CoV values assumes that variability throughout the production line would be "average," or "modest" – when, in fact, the typical coefficients of variability of the actual production line ranged from slightly less than 1.0 to well over 10.0

(i.e., *Excessive* Variability). [Much of that variability, it should be noted, was a consequence of their *non*-C4U-compliant maintenance specs coupled with an unawareness of the existence of, or familiarity with, the Waddington Effect [Ignizio, J. P. (2009); Ignizio, J. P. (2010a)].

Later, when a much less detailed (i.e., as Einstein said, "make it as simple as possible but not simpler") simulation package was employed to model the fab, and – particularly – when far more representative values for the coefficients of variability were used, the simulation model's predictions were very close to those of the actual fab – and were achieved in a fraction of the time. Had management realized the importance of those two matters they would not have been taken by surprise by the poor performance of their new facility. Or, even better, they could have taken the steps necessary to enhance its performance prior to the fab's construction.

The lesson here is that you should never assume that your processing units (be they in a production line, supply chain, or business processing system) are subject to "modest" levels of variability. Modest levels (e.g., coefficients of variability of 1.0) are not necessarily – and seldom are – the level of variability encountered in the real world. Furthermore, if you are blissfully unaware of the Waddington Effect, you are 100 percent sure to be experiencing it – to the detriment of the performance of your production line, supply chain, or business processes.

Just as you shouldn't assume "modest levels of variability," you shouldn't assume that *non-constraints* within a processing system aren't worth dealing with. This particularly important matter is addressed in the following section.

Don't Waste Your Time On Non-Constraints?

Senior management at a major manufacturing firm expressed their displeasure with the latest report on their factories' cycle times. Their cycle time goal had been set at 56 days. Instead, the actual cycle time was approximately 90 days – *and increasing*. Customers were complaining about late deliveries and it was taking much too long to determine the source of defects in the production line.

The firm's management decided to incorporate a recommendation proposed jointly by their Cycle Time and Capacity performance teams. Those two teams unanimously concluded – after a 3-day course on the Theory of Constraints provided by an outside consultant – that they could simultaneously increase their factory capacity and, they believed, *reduce product cycle time by finding and improving (i.e., increasing the capacity of) the production line's constraint (aka: bottleneck, chokepoint).*

> *Before proceeding further, notice that the problem faced by the firm was that of* **excessive cycle time**. *The Theory of Constraints, however, is focused on the increase in factory* **throughput** *by means, allegedly, of "alleviating" production line constraints. Also notice an even more important point. The Theory of Constraints, as shall be discussed in detail, is what is known as an* **atomistic** *method; i.e., it (narrowly) focuses on a specific part (i.e., the*

bottlenecks) of the system under consideration.

A core concept of the Theory of Constraints (ToC) is founded on the assumption that *every process has a single constraint.* According to ToC, product flow (throughput flow, i.e., rate of the flow of tasks per unit time) is only improved when *the* constraint is "elevated" (e.g., when its capacity is increased).

The *corollary to this concept is that there is no significant gain to be achieved optimizing non-constraints.* I'll discuss these two problematic beliefs in a moment. First, however, consider the basic steps of the Theory of Constraints:

- Identify *the single constraint* (e.g., the workers, part, machine, or transport mechanism that is limiting throughput)
- Increase the throughput (i.e., capacity) of the constraint
- Continue until the constraint is resolved and, if necessary, repeat the procedure on the new constraint

There are several problems with both the premise and steps of the Theory of Constraints. A particularly serious one is the fact that it either ignores, or at the very least underestimates the importance of variability and (in particular) the propagation of variability. But let's begin with its core assumption and its corollary; i.e., *every process has a single constraint* and *there is no significant gain to be achieved optimizing non-constraints.* (The fundamental problem, the *atomistic* focus of virtually all management and manufacturing schemes, is the subject of the next chapter.)

Having collected and/or evaluated data from

literally hundreds of production lines, supply chains, and business processes over nearly four decades, I can categorically state that there are many, many, production lines, business processes, and supply chains in which:

- there are *multiple constraints*, e.g., processes, which *at any given time*, have the same or nearly the same (limiting) capacities, *particularly in complex systems* (e.g., semiconductor fabs, solar cell manufacturing, certain business processes, etc.),
- *constraints migrate* (i.e., what may have been a constraint at one point in time may not be a constraint a short time later as a consequence of "WIP bubbles," machine breakdowns, personnel errors, etc.) – as anyone who has dealt with actual processing lines (e.g., semiconductor fabs) should know,
- in many, many real-world situations the "optimal performance" of the production line (or business process, or supply chain) *can be achieved* – faster and cheaper – by simply reducing the *variability* of one or more *non-constraints*.

Since I promised to do my best to avoid any esoteric mathematics or academic jargon, I refer the reader wishing to see the formulas and supporting numerical illustrations to Chapters 4, 6, and 12 of *Optimizing Factory Performance* [Ignizio, J. P. (2009)]. In those chapters, comparisons are presented in which the cycle time for a production line, consisting of 12 workstations (each of which has a number of machines), is reduced by either the "Greedy Heuristic," the Theory of Constraints, or simply by means of *reducing the variability of non-constraints*. In every instance, the reduction of the variability of non-constraints is far superior, in terms of faster and less costly cycle time reduction, than alternative approaches.

This result, the decreased cycle time via the reduction of variability within a non-constraint, is not a "one off." It is, instead, a general rule.

To summarize, while the Theory of Constraints may be employed to increase production line *throughput* (although, as we shall see, not always successfully), *cycle time* is most effectively minimized by reducing *variability*. Furthermore, *increasing the capacity of a constraint can actually increase cycle time*. This counterintuitive consequence will be discussed in the following section.

Another Example Of *One Plus One Is Not Necessarily Two*

"Everybody knows that, if you remove *one foot of rope* from a *ten-foot long* piece of rope, the result is a *nine-foot long* piece of rope." The previous quote is taken *verbatim* from the disdainful reply of a red-faced senior-level manager in response to an oral report I submitted to his firm.

The man's retort had been in reply to my assertion that, for their production line, *the reduction of the cycle time of one processing step* – **by means of the firm having increased its capacity** – *had resulted in an increase in* **overall** *cycle time*. "Impossible," said the man as he stood up and briskly walked out of the meeting. His remarks were, I suppose, those of someone who held fast to the belief that "the whole is equal to the sum of its parts."

Earlier that year I had been asked, by the same senior-level manager, to investigate what he termed "an odd situation" that had been observed following the implementation of a Theory of Constraints effort, coupled with a particularly intensive Lean effort, by one of the firm's factory performance teams.

The team had been tasked with an increase in the throughput (in terms of products out per week) of the production line. They had identified one particular processing unit (workstation X) as being the culprit; i.e., the factory constraint. That workstation, located approximately a quarter of the way into the production line, was then "improved" by the addition of two more machines (i.e., its capacity was increased) and a de-cluttering of its workspace.

Even though the capacity of workstation X had increased, and *its* cycle time had decreased, the result was an increase in the factory's *overall* cycle by more than 10 percent. I had explained that, by increasing the capacity of workstation X, the variability existing at that point had simply been propagated farther down the line ... and that propagation of variability had subsequently increased the factory's *overall* cycle time.

About a month later the manager who had walked out of the meeting called me to (sort of) apologize. The firm had run a series of simulations of their factory that showed that the increase in the capacity of workstation X most certainly did result in its increase in overall cycle time. He then asked, this time very politely, how could it be possible that an increase in the capacity of one workstation (and resultant reduction of *its* cycle time) could cause an increase in the cycle time of the entire production line?

I have had the same question asked by graduate students in business, engineering, and math, and by some very smart and highly experienced practitioners. The short answer is that the system (any production line) is nonlinear, i.e., one plus one is not necessarily two. The long answer requires a familiarity with the three fundamental equations of a processing system – and hold for production lines, supply chains, and most business processes. These equations are:

- *Little's Law* (i.e., equation): Determines the average inventory in a processing system as the product of its throughput and cycle time.

- *P-K equation*: Computes cycle time as a (nonlinear) function of batch sizes, the coefficients of variability of arrival rates and effective process times, the number of processors, as well as the availability and utilization of the processors.

- *Propagation of Variability equation*: Determines the *coefficient of variability of the tasks* **departing** *a given process step* and is a *nonlinear* function of the coefficient of variability of arrivals and process times, the number of processors in the step, processor utilization, batch sizes, and availability.

These three *highly nonlinear* equations dictate the performance of a production line, supply chain, and most business processes. They also explain why our intuition is so often wrong in our (futile) attempts to control such systems [Forrester, J. W. (2013)].

Like Ripples On Water

The Propagation of Variability equation (aka, the "Linking equation") plays a key role in the functioning of production lines, supply chains, and business processes. It also plays a key, *hidden role* in the consequences of the decisions made *in any system*.

Consider the results of tossing a pebble into a calm lake. You'll see ripples, starting from the point the pebble hit the water and then expanding across the surface. The impact of the pebble has caused a "disturbance," a change in the previous state of the water.

Decisions, particularly major decisions, are akin to ripples on water as they impact the existing state of the "system" (e.g., firm, organization, etc.) and are propagated through the "system." Any inherent variability in the decision made (e.g., *Unnecessary* Complexity due to ambiguity and/or *Excessive* Variability as a consequence of frequent revisions) will be propagated within that system. While little thought may be given to that propagation, it can and usually will result in a "disturbance" to the *status quo*.

In one firm I'm familiar with, a disgruntled member of the Board of Directors floated (evidently via leaks to the media) rumors pertaining to a reduction in the firm's workforce. That was followed, soon afterwards, by the firm's denial of any reduction. The "pebble" had, however, "dropped" and the morale of the workforce sank ... and a number of key individuals left the firm.

In another instance, some years ago, a seemingly

mundane decision was made to reduce the requirements for the approval of home loans. This resulted in what is known as "subprime loans" and "no doc loans" ... and in people purchasing houses that they couldn't afford. The end result was what was called the "Great Recession." The ripples of the decisions that created that disaster are still propagating.

In short, every decision – like every pebble tossed onto water – creates an impact beyond what we may anticipate. The propagation of that impact is amplified by *Unnecessary* Complexity and *Excessive* Variability.

Difficult Decisions

The illustrations discussed in this chapter, as well as the majority of the decisions that have been presented in this book, have been – by necessity – less complex than most decisions faced in real life. Despite that, the book's central message (i.e., the need to identify and then surmount, or at least mitigate, *The Three Obstacles*) still holds true.

In my classes and short courses (i.e., on *Intelligent Decision-Making* and *Manufacturing Science*) I typically present the attendees with three complex, real world problems. I ask that they attempt to identify, for each problem, the sources of *Unnecessary* Complexity, *Excessive* Variability, and *Intellectual Myopia*. For those readers that seek a challenge, three such problems are listed below.

<<<<>>>>

Going Green: The nation of Britain, like many other countries (except, evidently, China and India – two of the world's three most polluting countries), is concerned with climate change and the pollution that is believed to be causing it. Their Green Party continues to grow followers and pressure continues to mount to take action. In London – the nation's crowded capital – the smog now rivals that of Los Angeles.

Michael Gove, the nation's Environmental Secretary, has a plan. He is convinced that the root cause of London's pollution – and that in other parts of his nation – is the dirty, foul-smelling emissions of diesel and gasoline powered cars. Remove that problem and, he is convinced, the pollution will vanish. Gove's proposal – a commitment made in 2017 and similar to a pledge made by France – is that of *a complete and total ban on the sale of new diesel and gasoline powered cars by the year 2040.*

Identify what you believe to be the three primary obstacles. Before proceeding further, however, you should, at the very least, examine the references: [Biello, D. (2016); Jenkins, H. W. (2017b); Swinford, S. (2017); Sylvers, E. (2017)].

<<<<>>>>

Chase Those Bubbles! (This particular problem is a fictionalized representation, using fictitious names, of an actual problem in an actual firm.) The new, massive, costly manufacturing facilities of HiAnxiety, Ltd. have failed to demonstrate any significant improvement in factory performance over their older, less automated factories. Their cycle times (average time between the entry of a raw product into the factory and its exit, as a finished item) are not just unacceptable, they continue to increase. Defects are also increasing and, because of the long cycle times, not identified until far too late in the fabrication process.

Customers are deserting the firm and placing their orders with other companies – companies that still utilize older, smaller, and less automated factories. HiAnxiety's CEO is demanding action ... if the situation isn't fixed, heads would roll.

The Senior Vice President of Manufacturing, Harry "Hurry Up" Rush, met with the firm's factory managers. The cause of the problems in their new factories – problems that had increased product cycle time – was, according to Harry, that of the ever-increasing number of so-called "WIP bubbles" that seem to randomly appear and then flow – like unfettered logs on a cascading river – through the production line. The obvious solution, he claimed, was straightforward: when warned of an approaching WIP bubble, shift resources to the processing station that is next in the path of the WIP bubble. Harry assured the firm's senior management that such a temporary increase in capacity would dampen the WIP bubble.

> *A "WIP bubble" is a larger-than-normal buildup of WIP* [i.e., "work in progress] *at a particular point in the line. WIP bubbles result in large queues in front of a few tools, while other tools, sometimes even bottleneck tools, remain idle. A common goal in* [semiconductor] *fabs is to smooth out the WIP bubbles, so that all production areas remain relatively busy. Smoothing of WIP bubbles improves cycle time by reducing arrival variability throughout the fab.*
> [Robinson, J. (2008)]

The firm's factory managers complied with Harry's demands and established "Bubble Busting" teams.

Those teams, once warned of the approach of a dreaded WIP bubble, would prepare the next processing station in line for the bubble arrival. Workers supporting processing stations not in the path (or no longer in the path) of the newest WIP bubble would be hastily reassigned so as to support the endangered processing station. Operation-to-Machine dedications would be changed ... and the impact of the oncoming WIP bubble would, all were assured, be contained [Ignizio, J. P. (2010b)].

Your assessment? And why?

<<<<>>>>

Boom? The rogue country of North Korea, despite decades of pleading and repeated admonitions by our nation, has developed and tested nuclear weapons and, more recently (i.e., 2017), introduced intercontinental ballistic missiles (ICBMs) for their delivery. An assessment of their ICBMs capabilities indicate that they will likely achieve their stated objective: the ability to rain down nuclear bombs on the continental United States (or, possibly just as devastating and easier to accomplish, stage an electromagnetic pulse attack that will destroy much of our infrastructure, and ultimately result in the deaths of millions of Americans).

In preparation for your analysis, read the following references [Chabot, S. (2017); Bowden, M. (2017); Jenkins, H. W. (2017a); and Bolton, J. (2017).]. The *Washington Exam*iner article is from a right-leaning news source while *The Atlantic* story is from a left-leaning source. The two *Wall Street Journal* articles are from a center-right source. They each offer various threat scenarios and potential actions that we supposedly might take. While this is an excruciatingly complex matter, is there *Unnecessary* Complexity? Can you identify any *Excessive* Variability ... and *Intellectual Myopia*?

Chapter Summary

Management schemes that fail to factor in, or simply ignore, the obstacles of *Unnecessary* Complexity and *Excessive* Variability are unlikely to provide long-term, sustainable solutions. This is even truer when, in dealing with a problem that requires reduced cycle times, you employ a method that focuses on increasing capacity. Or ignore the vital importance of non-constraints. Or fail to recognize that variability *propagates* – and that its propagation can undo efforts to increase the capacity of constraints.

To fully appreciate this, it is necessary to understand the vast difference between a *holistic* perspective and an *atomistic* one. That difference serves to explain, to a large degree, the high failure and disappointment rate of most management and manufacturing fads and fashions. This is the subject of the next chapter.

For those readers who skipped ahead to this section, as I promised, here is a brief summary of the chapter's findings:

- The answer to the uphill-downhill mileage problem is 2 mpg.
- Fred's "simple little problem" can't be solved with the data he provided. If, however, we assume certain factors it can be shown that reducing variability is superior to increasing

capacity – in virtually any situation in which the goal is to reduce cycle time.

- Remember the new fab whose plant manager discovered, to his dismay, that its cycle time was far greater than had been predicted by their costly, time consuming simulation model? He learned that the coefficients of variability assumed in their models were definitely not modest. Once more realistic CoVs were used, the predictions were much more realistic.
- In the majority of instances the variability of a system is underestimated.
- The basis of the Theory of Constraints (i.e., existence of but a single constraint ... and a focus on constraints while ignoring non-constraints) is flawed. There are often multiple, migrating constraints and – *if you wish to decrease cycle time* – the reduction of the variability of non-constraints (i.e., rather than increasing the capacity of constraints) is almost always superior in performance, faster, and less expensive.
- It is quite possible to reduce the cycle time of one processing station and, in doing so, *increase* overall cycle time. This is due to the propagation of variability.
- The impact of the propagation of variability is almost always underestimated.

- Because of the propagation of variability, the consequences of initiating many management fads (including the Theory of Constraints, Lean, etc.) can actually *increase* overall cycle time.
- Not only does variability propagate through production lines, supply chains, and business processes, it propagates whenever a decision-maker (e.g., CEO, military leader, politician, etc.) issues an ambiguous decree and/or frequently changes his or her mind.

Now on to Chapter 8.

8. Bad News

Even though sugar was very expensive, people consumed it till their teeth turned black, and if their teeth didn't turn black naturally, they blackened them artificially to show how wealthy and marvelously self-indulgent they were.
— Bill Bryson (*At Home: A Short History of Private Life*)

The physician, his face a grim mask, had one last bit of advice. "Get your things in order," he advised. "You know, a will, a list of your assets, how you want things handled ... er, you know ... afterwards." I left his office, limped to my car, and drove home, a destination some two hours away. All the while the shooting pain in my left leg ebbed and flowed. The painkillers I had been given didn't really seem to be helping.

I spent the next two weeks "getting things in order." During that time, my allergies – to dust, pollen, etc. – began to really act up. My sneezing and sniffling got exponentially worst. It's bad enough to be told that you have no more than six months to live; but to have to put up with the nuisance of frequent sneezing fits added insult to injury.

I tried a number of over-the-counter medications. Nothing worked. I continued to sneeze – and the pain in my left leg continued to worsen.

My local physician, a general practitioner in the

small college town I lived in, was on vacation. Desperate to find some way to control my allergies, I made an appointment with the only physician that seemed to have an opening that week. While I had no control over the pain in my leg, I hoped that somehow, some way, I could rid myself of the symptoms of my allergies.

The physician was a woman; a woman I guessed to be in her eighties. All I wanted was for her to write out a prescription for my allergies ... something stronger than the over-the-counter medicines I had been using. All the physician seemed to want, however, was to quiz me about my health history ... and that of my parents, siblings, and grandparents. I answered her questions honestly, until she asked me about any new "problems" I might be experiencing. I didn't mention the diagnosis I had received a few weeks earlier. Instead I said that everything was fine, except for the worsening of my allergies.

She was particularly intrigued by the fact that, as a nine-year old, I had polio ... bulbar polio. I explained that I had no lasting effects; that I had made a full recovery. She frowned, picked up a pen and began to write out a prescription ... very slowly, very deliberately. Every once in a while she would pause, look at me, and then return to the prescription. Once finished, she handed me the prescription, along with some advice.

"You really shouldn't sit that way, with your legs crossed like that. Do you do that often?"

I had to admit that I did. After all, it certainly seemed like a manly way to sit.

"Well," she said, "don't. You're putting pressure on your left knee. You may think that you are over your polio, but there's something called post-polio syndrome. Keep sitting like that and you'll wind up with a pinched nerve. Trust me, you won't like it."

I took the good doctor's advice. That was more than forty years ago. I didn't have the terminal disease that the renowned specialist, and his team, at a world-famous clinic had diagnosed. Instead I had simply been sitting wrong.

Holistic *Versus* Atomistic

The unnerving experience cited above only served to strengthen my belief that, by viewing a matter *holistically*, you vastly increase your appreciation and understanding of the situation faced (i.e., problem, system, etc.). A holistic perspective emphasizes the organic or functional relationship between the parts and the whole. The elderly physician, bless her, that correctly diagnosed the cause of the pain in my left leg took a holistic view. She actually saw me as a whole person.

The specialist that delivered the erroneous diagnosis viewed my situation from an *atomistic* perspective, i.e., the belief that an understanding of the parts *is prior to* an understanding of the whole. Neither he, nor his associates, took much interest in me during the series of tests I endured. For the most part the entirety of our conversations consisted of their asking me to "turn to the left" or "turn to the right" as they activated a variety of probes on my leg. Their attitude was, since I had a pain in my left leg, they would focus on that leg and run as many tests as possible on it. I've got to admit that my left leg received an awful lot of attention. Expensive, but *atomistic*, attention.

When it comes to making decisions, i.e., to solve nontrivial problems, I am convinced that a holistic perspective (e.g., the concept and guidelines that underlie *The Three Obstacles*) is far more effective than an atomistic one. I am equally convinced that *one of the primary reasons for the high failure/disappointment rate of management fads and fashions is attributable to their atomistic approach.*

Consider, for example, the atomistic focus of some of the most popular management schemes:

- **Lean Management/Lean Manufacturing**: The focus of Lean is that of the "removal of waste." Typically, the waste that becomes the target of a Lean Team is that which is highly visible (e.g., cluttered workplaces, messy toolboxes). Quite often the results of a Lean effort are captured (as in the case of those who lost weight on a particular diet) in "before and after" photographs. The before photos show a cluttered work area, or toolbox, or office, etc. The after photos capture the neat and clean results.

  While the intent of such an effort is commendable – a cleaner, neater, safer workplace is definitely a good thing – too often a Lean effort fails to consider its impact on the rest of the system. As noted in the previous chapter, if the Lean effort serves to improve (e.g., increase the capacity) of one portion of the system, *while degrading the overall performance of the entirety of the system* (e.g., via the propagation of variability), its benefits may be more than offset by a degradation of the overall system in terms of an increase in cycle time. In other words, Lean – particularly as often practiced – is not a holistic approach.

An alternative perspective of Lean is that of creating, or maintaining, a certain goal (e.g., factory output) *while using fewer resources*. Once again, the goal of such a Lean effort is admirable. All too often, however, the focus fails to consider the larger picture. If the reduction of the resources results in either an increase in *Unnecessary* Complexity or *Excessive* Variability – or both, that may well override any benefits achieved via the consumption of fewer resources.

Note, however, that a Lean effort conducted under the umbrella of the holistic guidelines outlined in *The Three Obstacles*, could alleviate those drawbacks.

- **Theory of Constraints**: In the previous chapter some of the drawbacks of the Theory of Constraints (i.e., ToC) were detailed. These include:

    * A focus on the "elevation" of constraints (i.e., bottlenecks or chokepoints). This "elevation" is achieved by increasing the capacity (i.e., so as to increase the throughput flow rate) of the constraint. Such an increase in capacity, however, can – and

often does – simply allow the propagation of variability, and results (as it did in the examples) in increased *overall* cycle time.

  * A corollary of ToC is that there is supposedly no significant gain to be achieved by optimizing non-constraints. This is simply not true if your goal is, or as in most cases should be, to reduce cycle time. In such a case any reduction in the *Excessive* Variability within a *non-constraint* will decrease overall cycle time (while an increase in the capacity of a constraint could increase overall cycle time).

  * Again, if the ToC effort is conducted under the holistic umbrella of *The Three Obstacles*, its potential negative outcomes might be avoided or at least mitigated.

- **Six Sigma (and Lean Six Sigma)**: The primary focus of Six Sigma is that of the reduction of defects (e.g., mistakes, defective parts). The website, iSixSigma.com, defines Six Sigma as: *a disciplined, data-driven approach and methodology for eliminating defects (driving toward six standard deviations between the mean and the nearest specification limit) in any process from manufacturing to transaction and from product to service.* I certainly can't argue with that goal. Nor do I find anything wrong with combining Six Sigma with Lean – they both have worthy objectives.

What I do have a problem with is the atomistic focus of Lean, Six Sigma, and Lean Six Sigma. By implicitly ignoring the crucial importance of cycle time, *Unnecessary* Complexity, and *Excessive* Variability, Lean and Lean Six Sigma have, to use an old cliché, "taken their eyes off the ball." While it's important to reduce defects/mistakes, that should not take precedence over reducing complexity and decreasing cycle time. And it is a fact that Lean, Six Sigma, and Lean Six Sigma efforts do, sometimes, increase cycle time.

There is, however, another problem – other than their atomistic focus – that only further serves to increase their failure/disappointment rate. Before I get to that, however, perhaps it's time for a commercial.

An Offer You Can't Refuse?

I'd like to offer you a once in a lifetime opportunity. I deliver several truly amazing courses (each three days in duration) that may be of interest. Each course enables you to become a world-renowned expert in a variety of topics. Since you've been so kind as to buy this book, I'll even give you a discount. Listed below are three of the most popular of these courses.

- *Theoretical Physicist.* In just three days you'll become an acclaimed theoretical physicist, joining the ranks of such geniuses as Albert Einstein, Stephen Hawking, and Max Planck. Solve the world's most complex problems! Win the Nobel Prize!

- *Neurosurgeon.* You too can become an expert brain surgeon. Open skulls of the rich and famous while winning fame and fortune!
- *Author.* Learn to write as expertly as Jane Austen, William Shakespeare, Ernest Hemingway, and Charles Dickens. Sell millions upon millions of books! See each of those best sellers made into movies!

Have you decided on which course you'd like to take? Do you have your credit card ready?

Or do you recognize the absurdity of the claims for these "courses?"

Obviously, a three-day course isn't going to turn you into a world-class theoretical physicist, neurosurgeon, or best-selling author. Nor, sadly, will a three-day (or weeklong, or even yearlong course in those subjects) guarantee expertise.

So, why then would a three-day, five-day, or even a semester long course enable you to become an expert in such topics as Lean, Six Sigma, BPR, or Theory of Constraints? And just how could you expect to expertly *apply* any of these to serious problems in, for example, a massively complex semiconductor fab if you, yourself, haven't done anything more than toured its clean room, or perhaps read a book on semiconductor manufacturing?

While expertise in Lean, Six Sigma, BPR, TQC, etc. is hardly on the same level as that needed to be an expert in, say, theoretical physics, I hope you realize that their successful application requires a certain amount of intensive training, of a sufficient duration — and that any classroom or short course training should be augmented with an appreciation of the intricacies of the system in which you hope to successfully apply a management scheme. I also might add, at the risk of hurting some people's feelings, that not everyone will achieve the same level of proficiency in any given specialty – no matter how great their desire or how hard they strive. If that were not true I would have played center field for the New York Yankees and broken "Joltin' Joe" DiMaggio's 56 game hitting streak – instead of having a brief and mediocre Little League experience.

The lack of an appreciation of the training required, along with the atomistic view of most fads, are my major concerns with management fads and fashions. I have witnessed far too many attempts to improve the performance of a production line, supply chain, or business process by academicians or management gurus that have but a superficial appreciation of the system in question.

And yet it is evidently believed that, after viewing a few days of PowerPoint slides, the attendees of such courses are fully prepared to manage the successful implementation of the management scheme featured in such a course. Anyone who believes that has a serious case of *Intellectual Myopia*.

Black Teeth?

Before we leave this chapter, I should explain the purpose of the Bill Bryson quote at its beginning. Bryson said, in his book *At Home: A Short History of Private Life*, that "Even though sugar was very expensive, people [i.e., during the reign of Queen Elizabeth I] consumed it till their teeth turned black, and if their teeth didn't turn black naturally, they blackened them artificially to show how wealthy and marvelously self-indulgent they were."

Those who subscribed to this fad (i.e., black teeth) represent the extremes of atomism. The fad they followed focused on a single part of their anatomy: their teeth. While they may have impressed their contemporaries — at least those who bought into the wonders of black teeth — they did so at great peril to their health. The same is true of the advocates of management fads that are atomistic, rather than holistic ... and whose training consists of viewing a few days of PowerPoint slides.

9. Summary And Conclusions

Progress is impossible without change, and those who cannot change their minds cannot change anything.
— George Bernard Shaw

I've been asked if *The Three Obstacles* isn't just "another fad." The short answer is: *no*. The long answer is that each of the three obstacles exist in any attempt to find a solution to any non-trivial decision. They must be dealt with, and dealt with holistically, if a decision is to succeed.

There is a vast amount of empirical evidence, coupled with formal studies (e.g., of information overload) as well as countless results achieved by such pioneering management scientists as Frank Bunker Gilbreth, that show that a reduction in *Unnecessary* Complexity has *always* improved decision-making. Similarly, there is a massive amount of empirical evidence, clinical studies, simulations, and mathematical proofs that show – conclusively – that complexity induces variability.

There is a scientific basis (e.g., the P-K equation, simulation studies, clinical studies, etc.) that proves – conclusively – that variability increases cycle time and that any reduction of variability will always reduce cycle time while not negatively impacting capacity. It is also a scientific fact that variability propagates.

Furthermore, there are centuries of examples of the negative properties and unfortunate consequences of *Intellectual Myopia*. Finally, no one has, to date, proven that *Intellectual Myopia* has ever improved decision-making.

Guidelines And Recommendations

When faced with an important, nontrivial decision – needed in support of achieving a specific goal – the steps that should be taken are:

- If the problem is of any significance, assign it to your best and brightest (and not to those who, at the moment, either have some time on their hands or aren't engaged in any particularly important matters ... there's a reason for their ready availability).

- Maintain, at all times, a *holistic* perspective. Avoid the temptation to focus, exclusively, on only a part of the problem/system. Don't jump too hastily to a conclusion.

- Gain a solid understanding of the problem faced, list the choices available and the likely consequences of any decision that might be made.

- Determine as much as you can with regard to the problem's history and any previous attempts to solve it. Consider any analogous problems/situations and what may have been successful in their solution.

- Specify the goal (e.g., minimize the cycle time of a supply chain, select a cost-effective design for a new product, reduce the cost of a project, determine the causes of unscheduled maintenance, etc.).
- Identify *Unnecessary* Complexity and its sources. Then determine ways in which to reduce this impediment.
- Identify *Excessive* Variability and its sources. Then determine ways to reduce this impediment.
- Consider the possibility of the propagation of variability. Determine ways to reduce this.
- Present your recommendations to the decision-maker (and hope that he/she is not afflicted with *Intellectual Myopia*).

Too Much Of A "Good" Thing

I've referred, in previous chapters, to the importance of what I call the Waddington Effect [Ignizio, J. P. (2010a)]. During WW2, a British academician, C. H. Waddington, was assigned to an Operational Research group in support of the airplanes of the British Air Coastal Command. That command, in turn, was dedicated to the battle against the German U-boat threat.

A major problem facing the command was that of the frequency of *unscheduled* repairs by their air fleet. The frequency of these unscheduled downs, and the time required for the unscheduled repairs, was having an enormous impact on the fleet's readiness.

Conventional wisdom – particularly within the command's military leadership – held that, if their planes were so often down for *unscheduled* repairs, the answer was "obviously" to perform more frequent *scheduled* maintenance. So, if a preventive maintenance (PM) event had been performed every 30 hours of flying time, simply perform it more frequently, e.g., every 20 hours. It seemed so simple, so blindingly obvious.

Waddington was not so sure. He recognized that he was faced with a very complex problem (which, it was later proved, was *Unnecessarily* Complex) in which there existed *Excessive* Variability (i.e., the variability of the incidents of unscheduled aircraft repairs).

Waddington and his team collected data and even watched the maintenance crews perform the various PM events (i.e., they didn't simply sit at their desks). What they discovered was that the rate of the unscheduled repairs was highest shortly after a scheduled PM and fell to a lower rate until the next PM event was conducted, and then the cycle repeated itself.

In other words it appeared that the scheduled PMs were being conducted *too frequently*, rather than not frequently enough. That was confirmed by later experiments (in which the time between PMs was increased).

In addition to examining the frequency of PMs and unscheduled repairs, an investigation into the conduct of the PMs was undertaken. It was quickly found that any reliance on the "data" supplied by the maintenance crews was practically worthless and thus skilled observers were used to record the (correct and appropriate) data. The result of this investigation was an improvement of the maintenance and repair specifications (i.e., what I term C4U-compliant specs), and a subsequent reduction in the time needed to conduct them.

The interested reader or, in particular, anyone that deals with a firm's maintenance program, would be advised to read pages 60-71 of Waddington's book [Waddington, C. H. (1973)] for more details.

<<<<>>>>

While Waddington didn't use the terms *Unnecessary* Complexity or *Excessive* Variability in his writings, they were two of the obstacles he faced. He also encountered *Intellectual Myopia* as exhibited by the British career military officers who so routinely dismissed his advice. After all, what could an academician – one whose field of interest, for heaven's sake, was *animal genetics* – possibly have to offer in terms of advice to experienced, high-ranking military officers? (Actually, an awful lot. Just read his book.)

A Final Visit To The World Columbian Fair

In the introductory chapter of this book I promised to return to the Westinghouse versus Edison-General Electric battle to win the lighting contract for the 1893 World Columbian Fair. In this section of Chapter 9 I'll recap the discussion from Chapter 1 but, this time, the focus will be on *The Three Obstacles*. You may recall that Westinghouse won the contract for the illumination of the fair by entering a much lower bid. Westinghouse did so even though it was obvious that they would lose money on the effort.

The most frustrating of *The Three Obstacles* is that of *Intellectual Myopia*. One of the most common symptoms of *Intellectual Myopia* is a short-term vision, i.e., a focus on the near term. Edison-General Electric exhibited that symptom when they allowed Westinghouse to underbid them. Westinghouse took a long-term view, realizing that – while they would lose money on a winning bid – the (massive) publicity the firm would (and did) receive would overcome that short-term loss. George Westinghouse had his eye on the future. His competitor, on the other hand, succumbed to the obstacle of *Intellectual Myopia*.

While Westinghouse won the bid, the firm was banned from using the Edison light bulb. Thomas Edison was not a good loser. By prohibiting the use of the Edison bulb (whose patent would not expire until four years *after* the fair), Edison weaponized the obstacle of *Unnecessary* Complexity ... with Westinghouse as its target.

George Westinghouse could have given up, and allowed Edison-General Electric to take his firm's place at the fair, or attempt, somehow, someway to surmount the *Unnecessary* Complexity he was faced with. Westinghouse's solution was quite remarkable. Rather than chasing a myriad of potential solutions (and falling victim to *Excessive* Variability), the firm's effort was focused – for the most part – on one.

Westinghouse had, some years earlier, purchased a firm that held the patent on a bulb that was inferior to the Edison bulb. It had a much shorter lifetime and a single-piece design, and that single-piece feature would have undoubtedly been considered a patent infringement of the Edison bulb.

I suppose George Westinghouse could have adopted the most popular fad of that time: wearing rubber corsets and knickers (they were worn by both men and women and supposedly aided in weight loss as well as improving decision-making) but he chose a more rational course of action. He chose to identify and then eliminate two of *The Three Obstacles* he faced.

Westinghouse removed *Unnecessary* Complexity and avoided *Excessive* Variability by simply modifying the bulb it held a patent on (i.e., the Sawyer-Man bulb). Instead of employing it in its *single-piece* form, the firm constructed a *two-piece* bulb by simply gluing a ground-glass stopper to their bulb. While the bulb still had a short lifetime, that deficiency was overcome by manufacturing 250,000 copies – enough to fill the fair's needs *and* provide replacements for those that failed during the six months the fair was held.

Conclusion

The Three Obstacles are the primary impediments faced in decision-making. Unless the importance and impact of *Unnecessary* Complexity, *Excessive* Variability, and *Intellectual Myopia* are fully appreciated, and intelligently dealt with, those obstacles will have an adverse impact on the goals you seek to achieve.

As with any concept, the successful implementation of *The Three Obstacles* requires time, patience, concentration, and practice. Those decision-makers that demand a sure-fire, quick-and-easy, solution to their problems – without ever "getting their hands dirty," are unlikely to devote that time, patience, concentration, and practice. They are afflicted with chronic *Intellectual Myopia* and will likely continue to chase fads and fashions. Like Charlie Brown and the football, or the fad dieter – they will continue to wonder why any improvement that might be attained is so quickly followed by a return to the previous state of their system, or worse. Such an unfortunate – and unnecessary – result can be avoided. *The Three Obstacles* provides that avoidance.

References

Ashkenas, R. (2012). It's Time To Rethink Continuous Improvement. *Harvard Business Review* (HBR.org). May 8, 2012.

Biello, D. (2016). Electric Cars Are Not Necessarily Clean. *Scientific American.com*. May 11, 2016.

Bolton, J. (2017). The Military Options For North Korea. *Wall Street Journal*. August 3, 2017, pg A15.

Bowden, M. (2017). How To Deal With North Korea. *TheAtlantic.com*. July-August issue.

Brady, D. (2016). Tax Complexity 2016: Increasing Compliance Burdens Of Tax Code. *National Taxpayers Union (ntu.org)*. April 18, 2016.

Carlson, N. (2012). This Man Made $28,000 A Month Writing Fake Book Reviews. *BusinessInsider.com*. August 27, 2012.

Chabot, S. (2017). What Are We Going To Do About North Korea? *WashingtonExaminer.com.* July 31, 2017.

Chakravorty, S. S. (2010). Where Process Improvement Projects Go Wrong. *Wall Street Journal. (wsj.com).* January 25, 2010.

Clarke, P. (2015). Intel Orders 15 EUV Lithography Systems. *Electronic360.globalspec.com.* April 23, 2015.

Collins, M. (2015). Why So Many Management Strategies Become Fads That Fade Away. *Forbes.com.* July 11, 2015.

Cosgrove-Mather, B. (2003) IRS Can't Do The math. *CBS News.com.* September 4, 2003.

Del Angel, C. & Froelich, J. (2008). Six Sigma: What Went Wrong? *Forbes.com.* July 11, 2014.

Diamond, J. (2017). Pitchers Ditch The Windup. *Wall Street Journal.* April 13, 2017. pg A14.

Dillow, C. (2016). Only One Of Six Air Force F-35s Could Actually Take Off During Testing. *Fortune.com.* April 28, 2016.

Forrester, J. W. (2013). *Industrial Dynamics.* Martino Fine Books.

Gilbreth, F. B. (1909). *Bricklaying System.* The Myron C. Clark Publishing Co. NY.

Griggs, B. (2009). Could Moon Landings Have Been Faked? Some Think So. *Cnn.com.* July 17, 2009.

Harris, R. (2017) Dismal Science. *Wall Street Journal.* April 8, 2017. pp. C1-C2.

Hemp, P. (2009). Death By Information Overload. *Harvard Business Review (hbr.org).* September 2009.

Hopp, W.J. & Spearman, M.J. (2008). *Factory Physics (3rd Ed).* Waveland Press.

Houston-Waesch, M. (2017). First Job Of Dismantling Nuclear Plants: Find A Russian Speaker. *Wall Street Journal.* June 12, 2017. pgs A1 & A10.

Ignizio, J. P. (2008). The Yo-Yo Effect. *Fab Engineering and Operations.* Issue 5, November 2008. pp. 18-22.

Ignizio, J. P. (2009). *Optimizing Factory Performance.* McGraw-Hill Publishing.

Ignizio, J. P. (2010a). The Waddington Effect, C4U-Compliance And Subsequent Impact On Force Readiness. *Phalanx – The bulletin of the Military Operations Research Society*, Vol. 43 No. 3, pp. 17-21.

Ignizio, J. P. (2010b). The Impact Of Operation-To-Tool Dedications On Factory Stability. *2010 Winter Simulation Conference Proceedings*, Baltimore, MD.

Jenkins, H. W. (2017a). Nukes Won't Save North Korea. *Wall Street Journal.* August 2, 2017, pg A15.

Jenkins, H. W. (2017b). The Coming Global Car Wreck. *Wall Street Journal.* August 26, 2017, pg A13.

Larrick, R. (2017). Linear Thinking In A Nonlinear World. *Harvard Business Review.* May-June 2017 issue. pp 130-139.

Lehman, J. (2017). The U.S. Navy Must Be Everywhere At Once. *Wall Street Journal.* April 28, 2017. pg A19.

Loeb, P. (2016). PA Ballot Question Leads To State Supreme Court Confusion. *CBS Philly.com.* October 30, 2016.

McCrum, K. (2016). Moon Landing Celebrates 47th Anniversary But 52% Of Brits Don't Believe It Really Happened. *Mirror.com.uk.* July 19, 2016.

Miller, W. J. (1993). *Mapping for Stonewall: The Civil War Service of Jed Hotchkiss.* Elliot & Clark Publishing.

Niedzwiecki, S. (2017). ADAS Can Lead To Higher Insurance Prices. *glassBYTEs.com.* April 12, 2017.

Olson, N. E. (2017). Complexity Is The Root Of All Evil (at Least in the Tax Code). *Wall Street Journal.* May 18, 1017. pg A15.

Robinson, J. (2008). WIP Bubbles In Wafer Fabs. *FabTime.com.* November 12, 2008), Issue 9.09.

Roethlisberger, F. J. & Dickson, W. J. (1939) *Management And The Worker*. Harvard University Press, Cambridge, MA.

Savage, S. L. (2009). *The Flaw Of Averages*, John Wiley & Sons.

Shaw, E. (2016). Where Local Governments Are Paying Their Bills With Police Fines. *SunlightFoundation.com*, September 26, 2016.

Smith, R. (2014). Is Six Sigma Killing Your Company's Future? *Forbes.com*. July 11, 2014.

Speier, C. Valacich, J., & Vessey, I. (1999) The Influence Of Task Interruption On Individual Decision Making: An Information Overload Perspective. *Decision Sciences, 30*.

Swinford, S. (2017). Diesel And Petro Car Ban: Plan For 2040 Unravels As 10 New Power Stations Needed To Cope With Electric Revolution. *Daily Telegraph.com*. July 27, 2016.

Sylvers, E. (2017). U.K. Targets Gasoline, Diesel Cars. *Wall Street Journal*. July 27, 2017. pg B3

Tomlinson, L. & Griffin, J. (2016). Budget Cuts Leaving Marine Corps Aircraft Grounded. *FoxNews.com*. April 17, 2016.

Waddington, C. H. (1973). *OR In World War 2: Operational Research Against The U Boat*. Elek Science.

Weise, E. (2015). Amazon Cracks Down On Fake Reviews. *USAToday.com*. October 19, 2015.

West, M. B. (2017). Trump Takes Flak From A PR School. *Wall Street Journal.* June 29, 2017. pg A15.

Acknowledgements

The Three Obstacles represents, in many respects, a summation of the lessons I have learned over a career that now spans more than a half-century. Its philosophy, content, and message have been influenced by personal experiences, personal research, interactions with other researchers, and interactions and relationships with a host of real-world decision-makers – both successful and unsuccessful.

I owe a debt of gratitude, in particular, to students in both my formal classroom courses and those who have attended my seminars and short-courses. The questions they raised served to broaden my own interests as well as strengthen my conviction in the crucial importance of the recognition of the importance and impact of *Unnecessary* Complexity, *Excessive* Variability, and *Intellectual Myopia*.

All the above, plus ever-increasing evidence of the limitations of a seemingly never-ending parade of management fads and fashions, served to convince me that – while the book may be met with some degree of displeasure by the most passionate advocates of those fads and fashions, it is vital that its message be presented. Time will tell as to the impact of the book's message on those who read it.

Finally, I wish to thank those who have encouraged me to pursue this effort and added their input to the book's final draft. These include, in particular: Dr. William E. Biles; C. W. ("Bill") Klausman, II; Dr. Laura I. Burke; Darrell Woelk, and my wife, Cynthia.

About The Author

James Ignizio is the author of nineteen books and several hundreds of articles. He is a Fellow of the Institute of Industrial Engineering, a Fellow of the Operational Research Society of Britain, and a Fellow of the World Academy of Productivity Sciences. He is also a Distinguished Alumnus of the Department of Industrial and Systems Engineering at Virginia Tech and recipient of the First Hartford Prize.

Dr. Ignizio is Founder and Principal of the Institute for Resource Management. Prior to that he served as an Internal Consultant and Staff Scientist at the Intel Corporation, Professor and Chair of Systems Engineering at the University of Virginia, Professor and Chair of Industrial Engineering at the University of Houston, and Professor of Industrial Engineering at Penn State. He has also been a Visiting Professor at the Naval Postgraduate School, the Helsinki School of Economics (now Aalto University School of Business) and the U.S. Army Logistics Management College. In addition, he has held senior management level positions in the U.S. Aerospace industry.

Dr. Ignizio has served as both an external and internal consultant to more than 100 firms and his courses in Intelligent Decision Systems and Management Science have been attended by several thousands of individuals over the past three decades. He has also held the position of series editor (in Management Science) for Kluwer-Nijhoff Publishing and has served on the editorial boards of *Omega, Journal of Large-Scale Systems, Information and Decision Technologies, Computers and Operations Research, Journal of Multi-Criteria Decision Analysis,* and the *International Series in Operations Research and Management Science*.

Dr. Ignizio's primary interest is, and has been for a half-century, that of exploring the vital role provided by means of a holistic approach to decision-making. This book, *The Three Obstacles*, represents an attempt to present that topic in a readable and yet comprehensive form.

www.ingramcontent.com/pod-product-compliance
Lightning Source LLC
Chambersburg PA
CBHW052255220526
45471CB00001B/345